Don't Let Your Mind Stunt Your Growth

Stories, Fables, and Techniques That Will Set Your Mind Free

BRYAN E. ROBINSON, PH.D.

New Harbinger Publications, Inc.

Publisher's Note

This publication is designed to provide accurate and authoritative information in regard to the subject matter covered. It is sold with the understanding that the publisher is not engaged in rendering psychological, financial, legal, or other professional services. If expert assistance or counseling is needed, the services of a competent professional should be sought.

Distributed in the U.S.A. by Publishers Group West; in Canada by Raincoast Books; in Great Britain by Airlift Book Company, Ltd.; in South Africa by Real Books, Ltd.; in Australia by Boobook; and in New Zealand by Tandem Press.

Copyright © 2000 by Bryan E. Robinson
New Harbinger Publications, Inc.
5674 Shattuck Avenue
Oakland, CA 94609

Cover design by Poulson/Gluck Design
Edited by Carole Honeychurch
Text design by Michele Waters

Library of Congress Catalog Number: 99-75288
ISBN 1-57224-193-4 Paperback

Printed in Canada

New Harbinger Publications' Website address: www.newharbinger.com

02   01   00

10   9   8   7   6   5   4   3   2   1

First printing

*In loving memory of my nephew James Bradford Loftin—
affectionately known as Jimmy—
whose spirit and love continue to live on in
all of us whose lives he touched.*

Contents

Acknowledgments

I want to acknowledge the many people without whose help I would not have been able to complete this project. I want to thank my agent, Sally McMillan, for her tireless efforts in supporting my work. To Jamey McCullers, from whom I have received enduring love and support that is so essential to accomplishing a book of this magnitude.

My special appreciation to the individuals who shared their personal stories that became material for this book. A special thank-you to Sam M. Isenberg for sharing the story of Opti, the little sparrow, with me. To my friends about whom I wrote: Sylvia Brackett, Dr. Lyn Rhoden, Nancy Chase, Edie Irons, and many more, and to the people who generously gave of their time to read the manuscript and offer critical feedback: Nancy Chase, Stephanie Wilder, Kevin Davis, Richard Gershen, and Terry Souffer, and especially Jamey McCullers for tirelessly listening to me read passages and giving me constructive direction. My sincerest thanks to *Your Health Magazine* in which several of the entries in this book originally appeared in my monthly column, "Mind Matters."

To my teachers, my clients, and my colleagues in my private practice: Dr. Jane Carroll, Marty Claus, Kevin Davis, Karen DuBose, Jennie Holt, Dr. Edie Irons, and Dr. Valerie Mittl.

You have taught me much without even knowing it. Thank you for putting up with me and letting me learn from our daily interactions. To my students and colleagues at the University of North Carolina at Charlotte in whom I constantly see myself reflected. Sometimes I don't like what I see and sometimes I do. You have been wonderful mirrors for me, and I am eternally indebted to you for your patience and generosity.

To my family, those who have gone and those who remain, especially my sister, Glenda Loftin and her husband James, and my sister Lynn Hallman and her son, Eddie. Lastly, to all the river dwellers on the Suwannee River, especially to June and Ronnie Kirby for always making me feel at home, and Captain Steve and Jan Bedenbaugh for all the fun times diving for scallops in the Gulf.

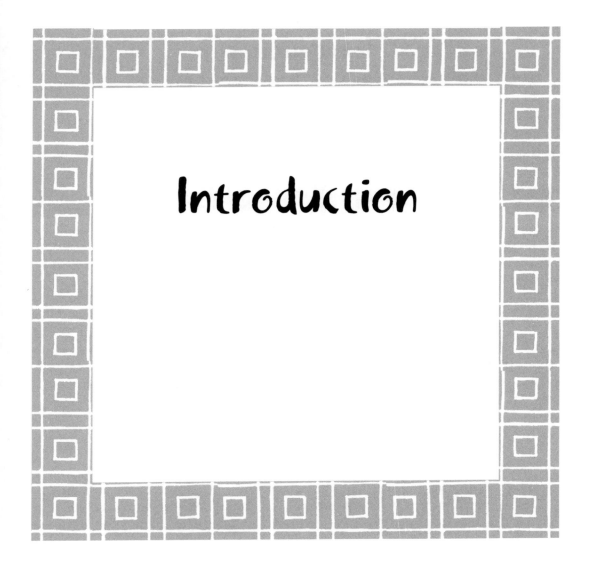

Introduction

Introduction

The unexamined life is not worth living.

—Plato

Once upon a time, I spent three weeks in Hong Kong, mainland China, and Thailand, where I immersed myself in the rich Asian cultures—the spiritual practices, spellbinding sights and sounds, and exotic smells and tastes of food. Upon my return to the United States, I found myself still immersed in the ways of the East. Shortly after my return, I walked into a colleague's office and noticed a book on her desk. My eyes glanced half the title of the book, which registered in my brain as "Tea-Ching."

Still basking in the enthusiasm of my trip, I pointed to the book and exclaimed, "Oh, I see you have an interest in Asian culture, too!"

She looked at me as if I were crazy and said, "No. I've never been there and have no desire to go, really."

I took a closer look at the book, and I chuckled to myself when my eyes caught the whole title, *Teaching in the Elementary Schools.* My Asian frame of reference caused me to bring a whole set of assumptions about this woman and her interests that were really about my experiences—not hers. These skewed assumptions were fostered by my Asian experience, which caused me to frame the situation with my colleague differently than I ordinarily would have. This small incident reminded me of how often and unknowingly we live our lives this way on a daily basis—bringing our own past experience to each new situation.

You also have a frame of reference, formed from previous experience, which governs the way you see each present moment. Formed from the words you heard and the attitudes, feelings, and actions you experienced from your parents and other significant adults, your frame of reference grows and develops, just like your arms and legs, from the time you are born.

Scientists at Cambridge University conducted experiments with kittens in order to show how the mind frames new experiences. They restricted the visual field of the kittens from the time they were born to only horizontal lines. Never having seen vertical lines in their early years, the adult cats could recognize horizontal lines (———) but not vertical ones (| |). They could jump on table tops but would routinely bump into the vertical table legs. Vertical lines were not part of the adult cats' frame of reference because they had never experienced them as kittens. The point of the experiment was to say that, because of their restricted past, the cats had a limited snapshot of the way they saw the present.

If you think about it, right now a million thoughts are going through your head. It's impossible for your mind to focus on all of them or to see everything in the room at once. So the mind has to restrict incoming information so that you can focus on one thing at a time. Another way of putting it is that your mind frames each present experience with a snapshot of the past, and you respond to present situations in the same way you did in the past, even though they really have nothing to do with each other.

During childhood your mind takes photographs that it carries into the future. The snapshots you carry—good or bad—make up your frame of reference, filtering each present experience. If you were a child who was repeatedly held to high standards that you could never reach, for example, these repeated experiences of not measuring up can restrict your adult beliefs about your capabilities. Children who are told they never measure up often develop a snapshot of themselves as inadequate, defective, inferior, undeserving, unworthy, or unlovable. As adults they are driven by these beliefs because the beliefs feel familiar. People go so far as to collect evidence in the present to fit their snapshots in an effort to confirm their deeply held beliefs. They are looking for the horizontal line, because that's what was shown to them in childhood.

Don't Let Your Mind Stunt Your Growth is a collection of sixty-four stories that encourage you to examine your life by paying closer attention to how your mind creates each experience that you have. Based on the principle that the ways in which you think about yourself cause you to feel and behave in certain ways, this book can help you change your feelings and behaviors by consciously and deliberately looking at situations with new eyes. In psychotherapy this approach is called *reframing*; in Buddhist practice it's known as *insight* or *enlightenment*. The Twelve Steps refer to an attitude of gratitude to recover from flawed thinking, or *stinkin' thinkin'*.

This book can help you answer such questions as: What past thoughts, ideas, or feelings frame my current relationships and experiences? Have these frames limited me or stunted my personal growth in any way? Do any of my present snapshots need reframing so that my life can run more smoothly at work, at home, or at play? Is there a person or situation in my life that arouses strong negative feelings in me and that might hold the key to ancient hurts?

The messages in each section contain meaningful, provocative, touching, sometimes witty ways to cultivate inner peace, satisfying relationships, and joy. They are written in simple, bite-sized portions so that they can be easily understood and digested by anyone who is intrigued—as I have been—with human nature. You can pick and choose which vignette to contemplate, selecting those that draw you on any particular day. As you reflect and silently apply each message to your life, you can imbibe it with a morning hot beverage, tuck it away in your mind and consider it on the drive to work, or read it before falling asleep at night. The selections are kernels of wisdom inspired by my extensive study of Taoism, Buddhism, and other Eastern practices; philosophy; the Twelve Steps; my training and practice of psychotherapy; and more than a half century of experience with life.

The selections contained in this book are by no means intended to pave the road of your personal journey but to provide a road map as a fellow traveler might, with hopes it can in some small way illuminate yours too. The simple and useful tools described here can prevent your mind from stunting your growth and help you see people and situations more clearly as they *truly are*, instead of how they *appear* to you on the surface. Using the techniques in this book can help you become more patient and more loving and experience difficult people and situations with less frustration and more calm. The simple messages that I share in this book have nourished and supported me in my seeking and have added much meaning and joy to my personal life. It is my hope that applying them to your life can help you gain insights, nourish and renew yourself, and cultivate a good heart and a calm, clear mind.

4

1

Start to Look at Your Life Differently

The principle of life is that life responds by corresponding; your life becomes the thing you have decided it shall be.

—Raymond Charles Barker

See Other People and Situations as Mirrors of You

The real voyage consists not in seeking new landscapes but in having new eyes.
—Marcel Proust

I was so excited I could hardly stand it, because I was on my way to become enlightened! Winding through the North Carolina mountains, my little car puttered its way to a Buddhist retreat center nestled in the Great Smokies. Although I'd heard about the wonderful teachings, I hadn't had a chance to learn or practice them firsthand because my life was so busy. But this weekend would be different. I would devote two whole days, along with other seekers, sitting cross-legged, meditating, chanting mantras, and contemplating the universe. I figured I would find inner peace and all of life's secrets would be revealed to me in one fell swoop. Who wouldn't be excited? I was on my way to becoming a "High Being"! And at the end of the weekend, I'd go away with the keys to eternal happiness and serenity.

A longtime friend and Buddhist had told me about this retreat center and had advised me that my experience there would mirror my everyday life. "Yeah, right!" I remember thinking, waving him away. "Gimme a break!" My life was so stressful and out-of-control—I'd be an idiot to go somewhere for more of the same. I was looking for inner peace and direction. After all, isn't that what retreat centers are for? To bathe you in inner peace? "He's just jealous because he can't go," I reasoned, dismissing the comment altogether.

But there I was—lost. Snaking around the treacherous curves, I realized I'd misjudged the time it would take for the three-hour trip. Having gotten started late, I hadn't left work early enough to beat the darkness. It was nightfall and I could hardly see the tiny, unmarked dirt road that curved ahead of me. I had left my glasses on an airplane earlier in the week, and it was starting to rain. I was already two hours late to meet my friend, Nancy, have dinner, and assemble with the monk who would give us instructions for the weekend.

Angry and frustrated, I cursed the darkness and beat the steering wheel. If only I hadn't waited so late to leave!

Hungry and exhausted, I finally saw the sign, "Southern Dharma." Once inside, I was informed that the other followers had already eaten and were beginning to assemble for instructions from the Buddhist monk. I scarfed down a bowl of soup and piece of bread and dashed to the assembly, the last to be seated. I was out of breath, my heart was pounding, and my hands were shaking. I had never felt such pressure in my life. My unpacked bags waited patiently in the car trunk and, although the other followers had settled into their rooms, I was homeless. The unsettling tension I felt was in marked contrast to the instant calm I'd expected. "When does the inner peace begin?" I grumbled.

Then the monk announced that beginning at that moment there would be no talking for twenty-four hours under any circumstances. My heart sank and my stomach pole-vaulted. "How could I possibly find my room and get settled without communicating with someone?" The next few hours were challenging to say the least. Every time I tried to ask someone for directions, I was hushed mid-sentence. Finally I was able to express my needs with sign language and get to my quarters.

It was years later in my process of self-understanding that I had to admit that my friend had been right. My experience at Southern Dharma was a mirror for me to see myself and my life more clearly. Before I had even gotten to the retreat center, the "mirror" said, "I can't see" and "I'm lost"—not just in the mountainous roads but in my life. Looking back on the trip, I could see that my old familiar friends—hurry, frustration, and anger—had car-pooled with me on the trip. Once I sat before the monk and he announced silence, I started to realize that two other frequent companions, anxiety and worry, also accompanied me. As painful as it was, I had been enlightened and didn't even know it.

Your life is a mirror for you too. If you're willing to open your eyes, look in your mirror and see what's there, every experience and relationship you have can reveal important information about yourself. As you continue to read this book, try to start looking at your life differently. Instead of blaming situations and other people for your unhappiness, as I did, start to ask yourself what your "mirror" reflects back to you. This practice can be the beginning of your cultivation of self-understanding, happiness, and peace of mind.

Change Your Attitude and Change Your Life

Nothing has changed but my attitude. Everything has changed.
—Anthony deMello

In my twenties I thought of myself as not much fun to be with and not having anything to say that others would find interesting. I would remind myself often that people just didn't seem to find me interesting. I would go to parties and behave in ways that fit with my attitude, standing on the sidelines while others laughed, danced, and partied down. Instead of joining in the fun, I waited for someone else to initiate conversations. But I never really gave them a chance. If someone looked at me, I would look away, driven by my sense of inferiority. After using this self-defeating behavior to prove my theory that folks just didn't like me, I would dejectedly take my leave.

Hindsight is 20/20, so the saying goes, and looking back I now understand why I was caught in that negative cycle. *Everything you do is a thought before it is an action*. This book started out as an idea in my mind. Now it's a tangible object that you're holding in your hands. If I had believed that I couldn't write this book, then you wouldn't be reading it right now, because thoughts predetermine actions.

Everything you create—from making a cake, redecorating a room, to changing jobs—starts out in your mind as a thought. The movie *Star Wars,* Beethoven's Fifth, the houses on your street—all started out this way. Planning to ask someone for a date, confronting a hostile colleague, or asking your boss for a raise are thoughts before they're actions. Even what you think about yourself will become true on a physical level if you believe it long enough, as it did with me in my twenties.

As I realized that my feelings of dejection were created by my thoughts and therefore my actions, I started to think about myself differently. I reasoned that I was as intelligent,

8

informed, and capable as most other people on the planet. As I began to affirm my positive qualities and to believe them, my behaviors in social situations automatically changed, too. Eventually, I completely disproved my old self-defeating attitudes, and people began to respond more positively to me.

You can put this simple principle into use every day, because you always enter situations with a mind-set that is based on your attitude toward yourself. Whatever you look for, you'll find. When you set your sights in a certain direction, you'll eventually see whatever you expect to see. This seems like a very simple idea but don't let its simplicity obscure its power and far-reaching possibilities in your life. If you look for misery, you'll find it. If you look for joy, you'll find joy. You create your experience of life in the things you find and hold on to. Whatever you look for is waiting for you.

When you expect a bad outcome, it can turn out that way simply because you'll think and behave in ways that fit with your attitude. Just as water takes the form of the vessel that holds it, your behaviors take the form of the thoughts that mold them. So doesn't it make sense that, if your experience starts with your attitude, you can start to change just about anything by changing how you think about it?

You can start with a negative outlook that stands in your way (for example, "If I leave this awful job, I'll never find one that pays as well"). Then replace the self-defeating attitude with a positive one (for example, "I can find a job that I enjoy, that challenges my abilities, and that pays well"). Write the new thought down in the form of a positive statement. Put it in a place where you can see it and say it silently to yourself often. Then start to take the necessary steps to make the positive thought a reality. And remember: It's not what life deals you that controls your happiness; it's your attitude about what life deals you that makes the difference.

Keep an Unmade Mind Instead of a Mind Made Up

If your only tool is a hammer, everything you see will be a nail.

—Abraham Maslow

A funny thing happened to me while I waited for a bus to the Honolulu zoo. I noticed a small red sports car stalled in the middle of the street and a police officer talking to the driver. The stalled car caused a traffic jam, and angry passengers leaned on their horns. A passerby walked over to check out the disruption, smirked, and admonished the officer for throwing his weight around and causing the traffic jam. This angry woman then stormed off, gesturing wildly and loudly proclaiming her dislike for cops. Instead of seeing what was really happening with an open mind, the woman framed the traffic jam to fit her preconceptions of police officers and carried her erroneous assumptions about the event away with her forever.

How many of us walk through life with our minds already made up about our experiences? When we do this, we don't see life clearly as it is, but only as we think it is. Made-up minds stunt our growth and cause us to miss opportunities to learn and love. We have expectations about events before they happen, and we face many situations with our minds already made up about the outcomes. Even when we're not aware of it, our expectations—already planted in our minds—influence how we view colleagues, friends, and loved ones, how we interpret their conversations, and how we treat these people every day. Although it is important to learn from experience, it's also important not to let preconceptions contaminate new experiences.

Because expectations are based on thoughts or experiences from the past, they can prevent us from seeing the world as it really is. When we carry those expectations around and apply them to the present, we enter situations with our minds already made up. Often when we expect a situation to turn out badly, it complies because we unconsciously think and behave in ways that will make it fit our expectations.

Scientists have conducted many experiments proving that we see what we expect to see. In one study, a group of adults was asked to observe a nine-month-old baby, playing with a jack-in-the-box. The scientists told one half of the observers that the infant was a boy and told the other half that the infant was a girl. Asked to describe the infant's reactions when the jack popped out of the box, the observers who thought the baby was a girl said she was "fearful." And those who thought the baby was a boy described him as "angry." The point of the study? To demonstrate that when we carry two different beliefs into the same situation, we *expect, look for,* and *see* two different things because our minds are guided by our two different sets of expectations.

We can apply these findings to the ways in which we approach life in general. We can create positive situations in the same way that we create negative ones—by thinking positive thoughts and behaving in ways that make them come true. Keeping our minds open to new experiences instead of making them up beforehand can actually work in our favor.

You carry happiness or unhappiness with you everywhere you go. You can create a better life for yourself by following a basic Buddhist principle: Treat your mind like a bed that you keep unmade instead of made up. If your mind is already made up before each new experience, then you're unteachable and can no longer receive insights. Unmaking your mind or emptying it of expectations opens it to receive the teachable moment in each new experience.

Start with ditching your old mental concepts and approaching new situations with an open mind. Give yourself the gift of a new mind-set, opening your life to new and ever-expanding possibilities. The unmade mind allows you to see your life more clearly for what it is, instead of what you think it is. The unmade mind found a cure for polio, painted the Sistine Chapel, and put us on the moon. The unmade mind can carry you to greater heights of personal awareness, happiness, and self-fulfillment.

Recognize the Thought Patterns That Make You Sizzle

◨◨◨◨◨◨◨◨◨◨

Men are disturbed not by things, but by the views which they take of them
—Epictetus

Sweat dripping from his brow, Mark had spent the entire day cleaning the house from top to bottom to surprise his high-powered, executive wife. He had grown up with critical parents whom he could never please and he had become very self-critical. He'd learned to try and overcome criticism by doing everything perfectly, and today he had no doubt his wife would be proud. She came home from work, kicked off her shoes, and sat on the sofa. Exhausted, Mark finished vacuuming and started to collapse in an overstuffed chair adjacent to her. But before his bottom hit the cushion his wife, pointing to a dust bunny in an attempt to help, said, "Oh, honey, you missed a spot right there." Mark went ballistic, accusing her of criticizing his hard work and screaming that nothing was ever good enough for her.

The same thoughts that frame our past also define how we see ourselves and react today. For example, during childhood our minds take snapshots of how grown-ups react toward us. Carried into the future, these snapshots—good or bad—become a filter for each present experience. Mark, who was criticized into the ground, developed a snapshot of himself as inadequate. Driven by this belief as an adult, he collected evidence to support it. In fact, Mark felt criticized much of the time—not just by his wife but by his boss, coworkers, friends, and even his children. He eventually realized that if he felt that way in most relationships, it couldn't be everybody else; it had to be partly him. And this realization was the key to change.

If we think of ourselves or certain situations in a fixed way—that we're unworthy, or a situation is dangerous—we'll take those thought patterns with us in our everyday lives and treat them as facts. We unconsciously superimpose those thought patterns, or snapshots, on current-day situations. Suppose you've had two heartbreaking romances. Chances are that you would approach the third with a certain degree of trepidation—a thought pattern that it, too, will be a heartbreaking love affair. Or perhaps certain personality types remind you of someone who hurt you in the past. You might catch yourself automatically reacting to these people with anger or harsh criticism, as if they were the actual ones who originally hurt you.

One of the things that makes me sizzle is when someone lets me down. My friend, Edie, and I made plans to go to dinner and a movie a month in advance. When I called her two days before our date to confirm the time, she had forgotten to put it in her calendar and had already made theater plans with someone else. Although Edie felt awful, my hair-trigger reaction was, "I cannot trust that you will do what you say. I don't mean much to you. I must not be very important." Her house could have burned down, and the knee-jerk thoughts would still be there, because they come from inside me, not from anything she did. They come from the disappointment over my father taking me to the movies and never coming back for me. I learned at eight years of age that I could not trust adults to do what they said, because that was what they demonstrated to me over and over again. And I've had this feeling in almost every adult relationship I've ever had. The good news is that I don't let those old disappointments get in the way of my new relationships anymore. I am able to see the old feelings as they try to creep into my new relationships, and I don't let them.

You can reframe old mental snapshots by paying close attention to when they pop up and prevent you from seeing a current situation as it really is. What you want to do is start to notice the people and situations that cause you to sizzle. Instead of automatically reacting, ask yourself what old, familiar feelings the experience is bringing up for you. When you do this, you'll see that it is usually an inner thought pattern that causes you to sizzle, not the present person or circumstance. This will allow you to see present moments more clearly and handle them in a more positive way.

Find the Hard Evidence
Instead of Mind Reading

Happy the man who has broken the chains which hurt the mind, and has given up worrying once and for all.

—Ovid

Wham! Bam! I felt like someone had slapped me across the face. I had just finished seeing clients for the day and had come out of my office. On a desk in the waiting room I saw some papers, a book, and a check that a client had neatly stacked for me. It had been the first session for the bright, corporate executive who came to me for stress and burnout. I had given her a book to read and some forms to complete for the next session. Obviously, she wasn't impressed with my recommendations and wanted to show it by leaving the suggestions I had made, along with payment for the session, as if to say, "Thanks, but no thanks!"

All week I wondered what had gone wrong. During dinner, driving to and from work, and out with friends I'd catch myself replaying the session in my mind and agonizing over how I'd misjudged what I had thought was a great session. Although we had made another appointment for the next week, I knew she wouldn't show. I found out that I was wrong all right, but not in the way I thought. She did show up for her appointment with a sheepish look on her face. Her first comment was, "I've dreaded this appointment all week. I'm so embarrassed that you're going to think I'm a bad patient. But I have to confess that you gave me so much to think about that I misplaced the forms and book you gave me, and I haven't done my homework. I've looked everywhere and can't find them!"

I laughed to myself. We had both made ourselves miserable all week for nothing. We had actually created problems for ourselves that were nonexistent, putting ourselves through needless mental torture! She thought I would see her as unreliable, and I figured she thought I was incompetent. We were both mind reading. This type of mental torment is one of the most damaging things we can do to ourselves. And most of us do it at one time or another. Mind reading is another form of transferring our thoughts onto a situation instead of seeing the situation for what it is. Based on previous experience and mental outlooks, we jump to conclusions about the outcomes of situations, and we project our beliefs onto them.

But can we read minds? No, even though we act as if we can. Suppose you meet someone new and after one evening out, they don't call again. Your conclusion? If you're mind reading you might think, "I guess I'm not very interesting" or "I'm not attractive enough." A month later you discover that this person was sick in bed with the flu for a week, and it had nothing whatsoever to do with you. You blamed yourself unjustly without any evidence. But the damage to your mental well-being has already been done, because you spent agonizing weeks thinking, "What's wrong with me?"

Here's another example: Your boss walks by your desk at work. You smile and nod. He looks straight at you and doesn't acknowledge you in any way. You shrink inside, thinking you're in disfavor or even hot water. You worry the entire week. Then a highly accomplished coworker shares a similar incident he had with the boss—evidence that perhaps it wasn't *you* after all. At a company meeting, your boss confesses that his wife and some employees have complained in the past that he gets so preoccupied with projects that he doesn't even see them—more evidence that you were not being singled out. The next week he gives you a glowing performance evaluation—final confirmation that not only does the boss not hold you in disfavor, but he regards you as a highly valued employee.

Again your mind reading was unnecessary and potentially damaging to your mental health. The way to fix this, of course, is to catch yourself when you're jumping to conclusions without evidence. Think of yourself as a private detective and ask, "Where's the evidence for this thought?" Sometimes you can wait for the evidence to reveal itself, but sometimes it pays to be more direct and ask the other person for clarification. You'll discover that 99 percent of the time, you won't find hard evidence to support your beliefs. The more you practice this approach, the more you learn not to trust your mind-reading thoughts and to suspend your mental outlook until the hard evidence is in.

Don't Make Negative Predictions Without Proof

*The foolish reject what they see, not what they think;
the wise reject what they think, not what they see.*

—Huang Po

How many times have you had a sinking feeling when you have to make a presentation, stand in front of a group of people, or perform in some other way? If you stop and think about it, you'll notice that the feeling comes from a voice inside you that predicts you'll mess up. Otherwise, why would you worry?

I've seen these negative predictions in many of my clients. For example, take Marcy, who had a series of panic attacks because she was telling herself that it was only a matter of time until she failed at her real-estate job. She said she felt like a fake and worried that the truth of her incompetence would surface and she'd lose her job. I was puzzled by the contradiction between her thoughts and the facts. She had just received an award and bonus for being the top salesperson in her company the previous year, and she admitted that others saw her as highly accomplished. Still she said to me, "At first I felt good about it, but then I realized it was a fluke, and it'll never happen again. So I feel like I'm going down the tubes this year!"

Not only did the evidence in Marcy's life not match her beliefs, it contradicted them. But instead of rejecting her thoughts and accepting facts, she allowed her mind to reject the proof and accept the negative thoughts. Unwittingly, Marcy was proving to herself that she was incapable, because that's what she believed about herself. If she hadn't interrupted the self-defeating thoughts, Marcy's success would have been marred by them, and her worst nightmare could have come true. But this story has a happy ending. Marcy was able to see how her thoughts were sabotaging her career and changed them instead of letting them change her. Today, she remains one of the top-selling real-estate brokers in her region.

This kind of fortune telling—the mind's tendency to predict negative outcomes despite contradictory evidence—is a common occurrence for many of us. When feedback from people conflicts with the images we have of ourselves, we sometimes interpret the feedback to fit with our belief system. In other words, we turn positive situations into negative ones. If you think you're inadequate, your mind will frame each new experience through that belief system and collect evidence to support it. Any situation that contradicts the belief that you're inadequate is discounted, minimized, or completely ignored.

The mind can be like an unruly child sometimes. When things are bad, the mind wants you to think it will last forever; when things are good, it wants you to think it won't last. Undisciplined, the mind can conjure up all kinds of scary thoughts that are nothing more than synapses firing in your brain with no real basis in fact. The key is to not fall for it, because every time you do, you go through the dreaded experience in your mind and emotions just as if it is actually happening.

Every time you catch yourself sending a self-defeating message, you can intercept it and substitute a more affirming message in its place. After a period of dedicated practice, you will begin to see a difference in your ability to think and feel more positively about yourself. During the next week, be on the lookout for any fortune-telling thoughts. Keep track of these negative predictions by writing them in a daily log without censorship. At the end of the week, look over your list. Star the ones with similar themes or that occur more than once. You may be surprised at how often you make negative predictions. These are the beliefs by which you live. They govern your feelings and actions. They tell you what you can expect of yourself, others, and life in general. Beside every negative prediction you listed for the week, ask yourself, "Where's the evidence for this prediction?" Not only will you usually find that there is no evidence for your prediction, but that the evidence almost always *contradicts* the dreaded thought. So what you eventually learn is that you can no longer afford to trust the negative predictions to prepare you for the future. Instead, the proof is in the pudding, and you can rely on that proof as your trustworthy guiding light.

Look at Your Life Through Fresh Eyes

A child's world is fresh and new and beautiful, full of wonder and excitement. It is our misfortune that for most of us that clear-eyed vision, that true instinct for what is beautiful and awe-inspiring, is dimmed and even lost before we reach adulthood.

—Rachel Carson

When I first set foot in Venice, I was dazzled by the beauty and culture—the aroma and flavor of Italian food, the priceless antiquities, the slope and design of the ancient buildings, and the romantic gondolas floating in the canals to the sounds of old-world music. On the second day I started to notice the cracks in the pavement and buildings and how hot and dusty everything was. By the end of the week, I had had my fill of Italian food, and the music had become old hat. After a few more days, I was fed up with the city. The uniqueness of the architecture was marred by graffiti, which I hadn't even noticed before. The beauty of the city soured as I began to pay attention to garbage in the canals and the rudeness of the people.

How many times have you started off a vacation excited about a new place only to find that by the time it's time to leave, you have a whole different feeling about it? The place didn't change—you did. Venice was still the same romantic, beautiful place when I left that it was when I arrived. All that changed was my view of it. And if it was only my view that changed, that means I could have changed it back by looking at the place through fresh eyes.

Many times, as we become familiar with an experience, we lose the fresh outlook we once had. Rarely do we keep the exhilaration of our first romantic relationship or the highs with which we started our first jobs or the enthusiasm with which we began parenthood. If you started to look at your life through fresh eyes, what would you see? The disappointments of another pressure-cooker day or the exciting challenges that lay ahead? Would you push through the day with your head stuck in newspapers, computers, and mounds of reports? Or would you begin to look at the people in your world as intriguing, engaging them in conversation and showing renewed interest in what they have to say? Would you snap at loved ones or try to be more tolerant and patient of their human frailties without trying to change them?

When you live each day as a first-time experience, something magical happens. Life automatically becomes different each day. You get a deeper appreciation for who you are and a deeper satisfaction out of your life. You gain a stronger respect for coworkers, loved ones, and others whom you perhaps ignored or took for granted. Just as I had my fill of Venice, it's easy to become bored with the monotony of everyday life. The thrill and wonder might seem gone, and we might feel as if we've seen and done it all. These are only thoughts and they can be changed. The key is to rediscover yourself and your life by looking at each new day in a new way. Along with changed thoughts usually comes a renewed outlook on life. You can find beauty in the ordinary, elegance in the simple, wisdom in the shallow, and excitement in the dull. The philosopher Teilhard de Chardin described this change as "ever more perfect eyes in a world in which there is always more to see."

You have the power to change your daily world simply by the view you take of it. You can *rediscover* the world that you have lived in for so long, and you can see that same world with new insight and greater clarity.

See Huge Blessings in a Big Loss

Our real blessings often appear to us in the shape of pains, losses and disappointments; but let us have patience, and we soon shall see them in their proper figures.

—Joseph Addison

The most memorable event of landing in Sydney, Australia at 8:00 A.M. wasn't the famous opera house or the harbor. It was being informed that, out of three hundred fifty passengers, I was the only one whose baggage hadn't arrived from Los Angeles. Red-eyed and exhausted after a thirteen-hour flight, those were not the first Aussie words I wanted to hear. Needless to say, I was heartsick. "Why me, out of all these people on the plane?!" I groaned. This was bad luck of the worst kind. Or was it? I was reminded of the teachings that I had been studying, which say that our real blessings often appear to us disguised as pains, losses, and disappointments. Standing in the lost-and-found line, I had great difficulty seeing anything positive about the experience. So I consoled myself by recounting the story of the Chinese farmer.

There is a Chinese story of an old farmer who had an old horse for tilling his fields. One day the horse escaped into the hills, and when all the farmer's neighbors sympathized with the old man over his bad luck, he replied, "Bad luck? Good luck? Who knows?"

A week later the horse returned with a herd of wild horses from the hills, and this time the neighbors congratulated the farmer on his good luck. His reply, again, was, "Good luck? Bad luck? Who knows?"

Then when the farmer's son was attempting to tame one of the wild horses, he fell off its back and broke his leg. Everyone thought this very bad luck. Not the farmer, whose only reaction was, "Bad luck? Good luck? Who knows?"

Some weeks later, the army marched into the village and conscripted every able-bodied youth they found there. When they saw the farmer's son with his broken leg, they let him off. Now was that good luck? Bad luck? Who knows? (deMello 1978)

Sure enough, what I had thought was bad luck turned out to be good luck. The airline gave me one hundred Australian dollars on the spot, and by the time I had eaten lunch and returned to my hotel my luggage had arrived. I ended up with all my luggage and a hundred dollars extra spending money to boot.

Things are never as bad as they seem. We can always find the granule of good in the bad when we look for it: more beauty than flaws, more hope than despair, more blessings than disappointment. It's impossible to always know which outcomes are the best for us. Once we realize that things happen as they are supposed to happen, we can start to accept every situation at face value and look for the message to be learned instead of labeling it "good" or "bad."

I challenge you to start looking at your life in different ways, from different angles. The next time you're in the middle of a letdown, uplift yourself by retelling the story of the Chinese farmer. Remind yourself that whatever the letdown is, you don't have to stay there, and that it will pass. Wait patiently, have faith, look for the blessing and you will see it. You can spend the rest of your life agonizing over what happened to you in the past or you can use the unfortunate experiences as opportunities to change your life and live it with quality. It's your call.

Recognize Your Criticisms as Reflections of Yourself

Most of the time, the trait against which we are reacting in another is something within ourselves that we do not accept.

—Alan Cohen

Once there was a farmer working in the field, when down the road came a stranger.

"I've been thinking of moving," said the stranger, "and I wonder what kind of people live around here."

"Well," replied the farmer, "what kind of people live where you come from?"

"Not very good," answered the stranger. "They're selfish and mean and not at all friendly. I'll be glad to leave them behind!"

"Well," said the farmer, "I expect you'll find the same sort of people around here . . . selfish and mean and not at all friendly. You probably won't like it here."

The stranger went on.

Shortly afterward, another stranger came along the same road.

"I've been thinking of moving," said the second stranger, "and I wonder what kind of people live around here."

"Well," replied the farmer, "what kind of people live where you come from?"

"Oh, wonderful people!" answered the second stranger. "They're generous and kind and very friendly. I'll really be sorry to leave them."

"Well," said the farmer, "I expect you'll find the same sort of people around here . . . generous and kind and very friendly. I'm sure you'll like it here." (Houff 1989)

The moral of this story is that when we react negatively to someone, often we are actually reacting to something within ourselves that we don't like. It has been said that the faults of others are like automobile headlights—they always seem more glaring than our own. Many of us have become experts at evaluating and judging others because it keeps the spotlight off ourselves. The fact is that the defects we point out in others are usually the very things we don't like about ourselves. Focusing on the faults of others is simply a way to distract ourselves from acknowledging that those same traits also exist in us and prevent us from seeing what we need to work on in ourselves.

The psychologist Carl Jung once said, "Everything that irritates us about others can lead us to an understanding of ourselves." I believe him. Sometimes I can catch myself on a fault-finding crusade. Once I step back, I can see that it's usually something within myself that I'm displeased about. Criticizing someone else is just a way to feel better inside. If I can highlight the defects of others, it makes mine more acceptable and maybe even makes me feel superior.

Try this exercise. Write down five negative traits that you can describe in one word each about someone you dislike. Then look at your list and notice how many of those characteristics also ring true of you. Your criticisms, judgments, and complaints can be more self-revealing than you may realize. The critical comments you make expose more about you than the person you criticize. They are valuable sources of information that can tell you about your own faults and what you could work on within yourself.

The secret is to catch yourself when you want to judge someone else and notice what the criticism mirrors about you. Then you can harness the energy you would use to criticize that person and put it to good use by working on that part of yourself. Once you've mastered this strategy, you can practice favor finding instead of fault finding and notice how much better it feels to elevate others instead of putting them down. This approach gives the other person the credit they're due and gives you the opportunity to gain better understanding, compassion, and a greater capacity to love.

Look for the Shades of Gray

Whether you realize it or not, there are no boundaries, but until you realize it,
you cannot manifest it. The limitations that each one of us has are defined in
the ways we use our minds.

—John Daido Loori

Thirty minutes through my sixty-minute aerobics class, I caught myself feeling tired after a long day's work. I wanted to stop and go home. But instead I told myself that, unless I finished the full hour, I was "a loser" and that I wouldn't get any benefit from the exercise. It finally occurred to me that I was holding myself hostage with this mistreatment, because it was clear that forty-five minutes is plenty of exercise.

Many of us think that there's something wrong with us if we cannot give a hundred percent to everything we attempt. This mind-set is supported by ideas within the culture that could be expressed in statements like: "I must be all things to all people or I'm a failure"; "I must be thoroughly competent in everything I undertake"; "I should be loved by everyone"; "If you can't do a job right, don't do it at all"; "If I can't do it all, I might as well do none of it." I call these self-defeating thoughts *black-and-white thinking* or *all-or-nothing thinking* because they ignore the in-between and blind us from seeing all our options. This kind of thinking prevents us from seeing the truth about ourselves and others, reduces our choices, and makes us feel trapped.

Let me just put the cards on the table here: There's really no other way to put it but that black-and-white thoughts are untrue. That means when you use these statements, you're being untruthful. And when you talk to yourself with these statements, you're lying to yourself. The truth is a dot somewhere in between the extremes—nested in the shades of gray. Suppose, for example, you tell your beloved, "All you do is complain!" I know that's an inaccurate statement, and I've never even met your loved one. He or she might complain a lot, but how can it be possible that someone complains *all* the time?

Perhaps the worst damage that black-and-white thinking can do is to stunt your belief in yourself. These thoughts can actually govern you; they translate into bad feelings and self-defeating behaviors. They tell you what you think of yourself, how to behave, and even how others see you. They can prevent your life from working the way you want it to. They can create stress, hamper your relationships, and undermine your progress toward personal goals.

When you get stuck in "all's" or "none's" and can't see the in-between, here's a strategy that can help you stop this self-defeating thought pattern and begin to see the shades of gray. The next time you hear yourself say the words *always, all, everybody* or *nobody, never, none,* it's a pretty good bet that you just heard a black-and-white comment. This is a cue for you to access what I call "graydar," which is really just a sensitivity to this kind of limited thinking where your antennae help you focus on the shades of gray instead of getting stuck on one end of the spectrum.

Once you become sensitive to the kind of language that signifies all-or-nothing thinking, you can begin to use your graydar to catch your black-and-white thoughts and write them down. Draw a line down the middle of a sheet of paper, making two columns. In the left-hand column write down any black-and-white thoughts. As you do this, you may be surprised to realize how illogical and untrue they seem. In the right-hand column rewrite them by substituting a more truthful statement. Here are some examples: "I must be thoroughly competent in all tasks that I undertake" becomes, "I don't have to be perfect in everything; I can take risks and learn from my mistakes." Or, "I can't do anything right" becomes, "I am competent and capable in many things." And finally, "I want to please everybody" becomes, "It's impossible to please everyone and it's unfair for me to put that burden on myself; my worth doesn't depend on everyone liking me."

After a period of dedicated practice of using your graydar, you'll begin to see a difference in your ability to think and feel more positively about yourself. And you'll feel like your life is working the way you want it to.

2

Make Thoughtful Choices

You don't get to choose how you're going to die, or when.
You can only decide how you're going to live. Now.

—Joan Baez

Choose Your Life Instead of Letting It Choose You

*Man does not simply exist, but always decides what his existence will be,
what he will become in the next moment.*

—Viktor Frankl

A situation that I witnessed firsthand six years ago has been a constant inspiration of the power of choice in my own life. A concert on the campus of the University of North Carolina at Charlotte featured ten Tibetan monks who chanted and danced. I was struck with their rhythmic musical instruments, colorful costumes, and their ability to chant more than one note simultaneously. But more importantly, I was impressed with their gentle nature—their ability to accept everything that happened without resistance and their complete unconditional love.

These qualities became very evident when a group of angry religious fundamentalists gathered outside the auditorium to picket the concert, claiming that Buddhists worshipped idols and that Buddhism was anti-Christian. In protest they joined hands and sang, "Jesus Loves Me." One of the monks came outside to see what the matter was. When he witnessed the disturbance, instead of reacting with anger or defensiveness, he approached the circle, joined hands with the protesters, and sang "Jesus Loves Me" with utter sincerity and love.

Dismayed by the monk's complete lack of resistance and perhaps realizing they had nothing to fear after all, the group quietly disbanded. My heart was deeply touched by the monk's gentle action in a way that it had never been touched before. I realized that this was freedom of choice in its purest form and saw how much such actions have to offer those of us in the Western world—if we are willing to embrace them.

Even more inspiring to me were the well-publicized struggles of Viktor Frankl, a concentration camp survivor in World War II. In his book, *Man's Search for Meaning*, Frankl detailed his confinement and brutal treatment at Auschwitz and other Nazi camps. Separated from his wife, starving, and naked, Frankl was stripped of human dignity and respect. Still, through all the suffering and degradation and the fact that other prisoners were dropping dead like flies around him, Frankl saw choices for himself each day. Alone, starving, and freezing, he was convinced that, though the Nazis could take away all the outer conditions of his life, they couldn't rob him of his inner resources—his will to live, his inner being, his spirit. So in a paradoxical way, despite the outer conditions of his life, Frankl was free. And this inner freedom helped him survive the Holocaust, find meaning in his personal tragedy, and develop renewed satisfaction and purpose in life. He had decided to choose life instead of letting it choose him.

The actions of the Buddhist monk and Viktor Frankl can be an inspiration to all of us. No matter how difficult things get in our daily lives, we always have the freedom to choose. Instead of letting circumstances make decisions for us, we can always decide what we think, how we feel, and how we will act in each situation.

Ask yourself a few questions. Are you making free choices in your life? Or do you feel like a prisoner of your circumstances? Are you condemned to unhappiness because of the hand life has dealt you? If you discover that your life conditions are controlling you instead of you controlling them, you may feel as though you are in an emotional prison. The power of choice is within you and connecting with that powerful part of yourself can make you feel completely in charge of your life. If Victor Frankl had choices in his hardships, then surely you and I have choices in ours. The Tibetan monk's actions also showed me that in the face of adversity, I can choose my feelings in situations instead of letting them choose me.

Making choices is like breathing. It's automatic. You make them every second of your life without thinking about it. If your life is not the way you'd like it to be, you *can* change it. The key is to become more aware that you have choices even in situations where you think you don't, to make conscious choices, and to take responsibility for the choices you make. Even *not* taking action is a choice. Ask yourself what choices you've been making that you hadn't noticed before now. The more you start making conscious choices in your life, the more in charge and happier you'll be.

Welcome Adversity as Your Friend

Adversity is our dear friend. It is the driving force that pushes us out of our comfortable nest and forces us to learn to fly on our own.

—Alan Cohen

You probably think I'm off my rocker for suggesting that you welcome adversity as you would a friend. Most of us run from adversity like scared rabbits, myself included. I'm not suggesting that you look for trouble. But when the day-to-day adversities find you (and they surely will!), try making them work in your favor by befriending them. How many times, for example, have you found yourself engaged in an unspoken power struggle with colleagues, sales clerks, public servants, or family and friends and reacted negatively to them? When you welcome adversity, it gives you an opportunity to take a proactive instead of a reactive stand.

Here's an example from my own life to illustrate what I mean. Years ago I shopped at a local store where I frequently encountered a sales clerk who was gruff and rude. No matter how nice I was, she was still discourteous. I tried smiling or asking her about her day. Nothing worked. One day, fed up with her sour attitude, I snapped back at her. Of course, that only aggravated the situation and caused her to explode back at me.

Then one day I read about the newspaper columnist Sydney Harris, who shared an unpleasant experience while shopping with a friend (Powell 1969). The friend approached a newsstand to purchase a newspaper and politely greeted the sales clerk who was gruff and rude. The clerk shoved the paper into the friend's stomach, to which the friend smiled and kindly wished the sales clerk a good day. Harris asked his friend if he was always so nice to the rude clerk and the friend said yes. Confused that his friend didn't react to the unkind treatment, Harris asked his friend if the clerk was always that rude and the friend said yes. His friend explained that he didn't want the clerk to decide how he would act and that he would make his own choices about his behavior instead of reacting predictably to the clerk's conduct.

The next time you get caught in this type of uncomfortable interchange, try *acting* instead of *reacting*. Reacting to situations is a knee-jerk behavior like the stimulus-response of a test-tube organism that doesn't have the ability to think. My reaction to the store clerk was as mindless as a single-celled organism being controlled by the conditions of my life. Reacting is a defensive stance that keeps you at the mercy of your circumstances; whereas, acting is a proactive stance that puts you in charge of yourself. When you think and then act, you are using higher-level thinking—the gift of the human mind—to make conscious choices that put you in charge of most situations.

Sydney Harris's story taught me that I had been caught in a negative web of reacting to the sales clerk and giving her the decision-making power over my life. It showed me that adversity can help me be strong instead of falling prey to other people's short-temperedness, hostility, and pettiness. From that day on, I made a pact with myself to act instead of react in the face of adversity. And you know what? This strategy made me stronger, more self-assured, and more in charge of my life. I no longer let the clerk or any-one else's attitude or low mood decide my actions for me. Instead, I am learning to stay positive when someone else is negative, calm when someone else is frantic, polite when someone else is rude. In each case I'm choosing how I want to respond. That choice puts me in charge and enables me to turn the tone of the situation completely around to my advan-tage. There's empowerment in that ability.

Try taking your small, daily adversities and reworking them in your mind until you can see them in a more positive light. Take an inventory of the adversities in your life over the next few days. Notice if you're wandering through life mindlessly, reacting to whatever befalls you. Or if you're using your full human potential to make thoughtful decisions, regardless of the conditions of your life. In other words ask yourself if you're *reacting* like a single-celled organism or *acting* like a human being.

Choose Calm Over Chaos

Freedom means choosing your burdens.

—Hephzibah Menuhim

Famished and exhausted, I had just finished teaching a late-night class at the university. It was 8:00 P.M., and my heart, soul, and taste buds were set on pizza. I figured that if I waited until I drove the twenty minutes home, it would be another thirty minutes before it got delivered. So I called from my office and asked that it be delivered to my house. They said it would be twenty minutes. As I hung up the phone, I realized that I had barely enough time to get home and meet the delivery person. I slung my backpack over my shoulder and made a mad dash out the door and across campus to my car—leaving a whirlwind of papers flying, doors slamming, keys rattling, and students wondering what the crisis was all about.

Driving like a madman, I felt the adrenaline pump through my veins faster than the eighty miles an hour that the car was traveling. I screeched to a halt in front of my house just as the delivery boy rang my doorbell. Arms trembling, heart pounding, and legs weak from exhaustion, I paid him and walked into my house embracing my pizza and asking myself, "What price had I just paid for dinner?" The answer was "a piece of my life."

By now you might be thinking, "This man must be crazy!" And in a way, I suppose I was at the time. I had taken a fairly simple dilemma and turned it into an uproar. Had I used forethought, I could have prepared a sandwich earlier in the day. Or I easily could have grabbed dinner on campus before my evening class. Clearly, I was acting blindly and irresponsibly by allowing the situation to override my peace of mind instead of using my freedom to make conscious, healthy choices for myself. Jean-Jacques Rousseau once said, "Man is born free, and everywhere he is in chains." Looking at my behavior in the pizza story and other episodes in my life, I began to realize how often I imprisoned myself by my own actions.

Sometimes we get so used to living with stress and chaos that it becomes a habit, and we find ourselves adding stress to our lives, even when we don't have to. Still we are all free to reject crisis and chaos and all unhealthy burdens, even though we may not exercise that freedom. And we are free to create better conditions for ourselves. How often do we turn a simple situation into a crisis without even thinking about it? Why do we feel like we are constantly putting out fires? Because we are constantly creating them. We can ask ourselves what we gain from these crises. Comfort? Success? Importance? Once we know, we can find more constructive ways of getting the same satisfaction. Creating crisis and chaos is nothing more than a habit that can be changed simply by becoming aware of how often we do it.

One of the things you can do is to become aware of how easy it is to take a simple event and turn it into a crisis. Ask yourself what you gain from such actions. Whatever these gains are, try to get them met through healthier ways that bring no emotional harm to yourself or others. When you find yourself in a potentially explosive situation—whether you are ordering a pizza or facing an upset coworker—whisper to yourself, "I'm choosing calm over chaos." When someone drives too slowly, things don't happen as promised, or someone is inconsiderate or rude, you can always choose calm over chaos.

Nowadays I avoid chaos by pacing myself for my own peace of mind and for the sake of my family, friends, and colleagues. One strategy that has worked for me over the years and one that can work for you in a tense situation where you want to stay calm is to think of an uproar as a spaceship taking off. See the person or event soaring skyward and visualize yourself staying on the launch pad. You never even have to get on the space craft, much less fly to space. This technique helps you choose calm while things around you are falling apart.

Using this approach, you are choosing your moods instead of letting them choose you. And when you do this, you emancipate yourself from the emotional bondage that can rob you of your freedom to decide.

Make the Best of What You've Got

Our greatest happiness does not depend on the condition of life in which chance has placed us, but is always the result of a good conscience, good health, occupation, and freedom in all just pursuits.

—Thomas Jefferson

In his book, *The Art of Happiness* (Dalai Lama and Cutler 1998), the Dalai Lama tells of two contrasting life situations to illustrate his point that happiness is determined more by our state of mind than by external events. The first situation was a woman who prospered from a financial windfall as a result of a profitable business investment. Her meteoric success suddenly gave her lots of money, free time, and retirement at a young age. After the dust settled from her newfound wealth, things returned to normal, and the woman said she was no happier than before the windfall.

Contrast her situation to a second one in which a man of about the same age was informed that he had HIV. Devastated at the news, the young man spent a year getting over the shock and disbelief. But, taking the opportunity to explore spirituality for the first time, he found his life transformed in positive ways. He seemed to get more out of each day than ever before, and he felt happier than he had in his entire life.

Material gain—a new house, car, or money—can bring us temporary highs that usually flatten out after a short period of time. Tragedy or loss can put us at an all-time low for a while. But eventually our moods rise back to normal. Regardless of highs and lows, there is a baseline of happiness that most of us keep going back to. So if we keep returning to a certain baseline regardless of our life conditions, what determines our level of happiness? It is our state of mind—our internal conditions—that keeps us steady in a sea of ups and downs and carries us over the long haul.

In contrast to the man who was transfigured by his diagnosis of HIV, there are those victims of life who choose to endure instead of surmount life's hardships. Take Katherine, who went to her boss and complained that the new employee with whom she shared an office made her nervous because she talked too much. Although Katherine had the reputation of being a complainer, when she asked her supervisor to move the office-mate to another space, he promptly did. Two weeks later, Katherine moaned that her second office-mate made her mad because she was so messy. Again the supervisor accommodated her request to move the messy newcomer. After two more episodes of complaining and moving, it became clear to the supervisor that the problem belonged to Katherine, not the four office-mates he had shuffled around to accommodate her. Katherine blamed others for her feelings, refused to deal with problems in a mature way, and depended upon others to solve her problems. The supervisor, by overaccommodating Katherine, supported her "victim" behavior and unknowingly stunted her growth.

All of us are confronted with problems at one time or another. The important thing is what we do with them. We are given life, but we have the power to create our experience of that life. When misfortune hit, the man afflicted with HIV refused to become a victim, turning his obstacle into an opportunity to become an *active* participant in life rather than just a *passive* recipient. He transformed his would-be tragedy into something that worked. Many situations bring worry and concern, but we don't have to take them lying down. We can think and act like a victim or we can find the granule of opportunity, no matter how small, to strengthen and teach ourselves to live a life of quality.

Although it's a challenge to see the silver lining in a cloud, it becomes easier with practice. What you want to do is to pinpoint the challenge contained in each negative experience you have. Ask yourself, "What can I manage or overcome here?" and "How can I turn this situation around to my advantage?" Start to make it a goal to use every experience—no matter how painful or difficult, big or small—as a lesson from which to grow. Change the labels you hang on situations so that the new tags put the hardship into a more positive and workable light. Try to create a no-lose, no-victim situation, and you will notice that the winning vantage point will empower you to live each day with hope and happiness.

Look on the Positive Side

'Twixt the optimist and pessimist the difference is droll: The optimist sees the doughnut but the pessimist sees the hole.

—McLandburgh Wilson

Once upon a time there was a little sparrow named Opti, who dreaded flying south for the winter. He put the journey off until winter set in, and it became so bitterly cold that Opti wouldn't live if he stayed any longer. So he finally took off and started to fly south. Shortly thereafter, it began to rain, and ice began to form on his little wings. The weight of the ice eventually made it impossible to stay airborne. Exhausted and near death from the cold, Opti's wings finally gave way, and he plummeted to the ground in the middle of a barnyard. As he took what he thought was his last breath, a horse walked out of the barn and proceeded to cover the little bird with dung. At first Opti felt that the horse had added insult to injury. "What a terrible way to die!" he thought, "to suffocate in a mountain of horse dung!" But as the fertilizer started to sink into his feathers, it warmed him and life began to return to his body. Opti also found that he had enough room to breathe. Suddenly Opti was so happy that he started to sing. The moral to this story is twofold. Not everyone who dumps on you is your enemy, and when you're warm and comfortable—no matter *where* it is—you can look at the positive side and be grateful for what you have.

The ways we choose to look at situations determine our happiness and peace of mind, not the conditions themselves. Every situation contains good and bad; you can look at the positive side or the negative side. When you hit forty, you can see your life as half over or as having half still to go. When you enter a rose garden, you can be repelled by the thorns or drawn by the beauty and fragrance of the flowers. When you hear the weather forecast of 50 percent chance of rain, you can realize that there's also a 50 percent chance that it will not rain.

There is a strong case for choosing optimism over pessimism. Research has shown that optimists live happier lives, have fewer health problems, and actually live longer than pessimists. Scientists know that your mind influences every cell because thoughts activate hormones that carry information throughout your body. Think of it this way. Your cells are constantly eavesdropping on your thoughts and are being changed by them. Every time you have a thought or feeling, every cell of your body creates chemicals called neuropeptides that carry information throughout your body and that directly affect you physically. Through the action of these neuropeptides, you become the recipient of your own love and joy or frustration and rage.

The stress psychologist Hans Selye (1956) long ago explained how the body manufactures its own poisons when under siege by negative emotions. When you are overly stressed, for example, your brain sends that message to your body through cortisol and adrenaline, stress hormones that can wear down your immune system, making you more vulnerable to illness. High stress and pessimism also have been linked to other body-chemistry changes that are believed to produce cancerous cells. So negative thoughts and moods cause your body to secrete chemicals that can physically harm you, potentially thereby shortening your life. Optimistic thoughts, on the other hand, can create body chemistry that boosts your immune system by increasing the number of disease-fighting immune cells. Optimism in the form of laughter and humor activate the secretion of endorphins, the body's natural painkiller, which help reduce pain and produce interleukins and interferons, powerful cancer-fighting drugs. In short, pessimism can make you physically sick and kill you; whereas optimism can heal and sustain you. As you embrace more optimism and joy, you can be happier, healthier, and live longer.

So doesn't it make more sense to start the day on an optimistic note, with hope instead of despair, helping instead of discouraging, with a smile instead of a frown? In the next few days think of some instances in your life in which you have focused on the negative side. Make a deliberate effort to look at the other side of the coin and notice what happens. Look at things through realistic but optimistic eyes. Think positive thoughts, feel positive feelings, expect positive outcomes, and create happiness and health for yourself.

Write Criticism a Letter and Tell Him to Leave You Alone

Sometimes I want to write criticism a letter and tell him to leave me alone. The problem is that when I don't see him for a while, I start to miss him.

—Ruth Gendler

Although I don't see myself as particularly critical, there have been times when I let loose with unbridled criticism, only to be met with bewildered silence. Once while on vacation, I went to a natural food store and struck up a conversation with the owner. What started off as a great chat ended in my being overbearing and critical of a concert pianist whom both of us had seen perform recently. To my astonishment I found myself counter each of her accolades with criticisms. Although I didn't like what I heard coming out of my mouth, I couldn't stop the litany of negatives. Suddenly, the free-flowing and lighthearted conversation turned stone cold. The smiles and laughter died, replaced by downturned lips. Fond glances turned into blank stares. The owner had totally disconnected from me, and I couldn't blame her. I carried an unsettled feeling about my unfair judgments for the remainder of the day.

For many of us, critical attitudes are constant companions. What would be left of us without them? How would we operate from day to day? Some of us carry a magnifying glass, looking for flaws and defects. We are critical of others, berate ourselves, and see enemies in the faces of strangers. But critical harangues and diatribes make us feel bad physically and emotionally. And they turn other people away from us.

Try this exercise. Name several one-word adjectives that describe how you think your loved ones might see you when you're in a critical mode. Mine might describe me like this: controlling, critical, hardheaded, know-it-all. Then ask yourself how *you* would react to someone with these same traits. I would probably react with annoyance, impatience, and frustration. I might even be guarded and keep my distance from that person. And this is exactly how many of the people in my life have actually felt and behaved toward me. Do your reactions match the way your friends and loved ones treat you when you're in a critical mode? If you're honest, this simple exercise can tell you a lot about how you could be keeping others at arm's length.

Almost all of us can catch ourselves being unduly critical at times and change it. "Why?" you might ask. Because it can give you clearer insights into the people and situations in your life, make you feel better, attract people to you instead of repel them from you, and get people to heed and honor your requests in business and personal relationships. Criticism is a bad habit that you can break through conscious efforts. Here are several ways you can modify your critical nature.

First, start to see your criticisms as desires stated in a negative way. What you want to do is turn criticisms inside out and expose the hidden desire. For instance, when you want a procrastinator at work to stop holding everybody else back, replace the critical comment of, "You never complete your work on time and you're holding everybody back!" with the desire of, "It makes things go smoother when each of us keeps our end of the bargain and meets the deadlines we set." When you want your spouse to keep a cleaner kitchen, say something like, "I love it when you put dishes in the dishwasher instead of leaving them in the sink" instead of, "How many times have I asked you to stop piling dishes in the sink?"

Second, use the Positive-Negative-Positive (PNP) technique. There are times when most of us need to give someone critical feedback. The PNP technique allows you to do that in a way that is honest and direct and that allows others to hear you without getting defensive. It softens your critical comments by sandwiching negative comments between two positives. It might sound something like this: "This report has a lot of merit. I would change the wording in the last paragraph. But overall you've done a great job!"

Third, make a pact with yourself to dole out three genuinely praising comments per day. This will attune your critical eye to the positives around you. And it gives you practice in finding favor instead of finding fault.

Stop Repeating the Same Actions and Expecting Different Results

Your subconscious mind works through the creative law which responds to the nature of your thought, bringing about conditions, experiences and events in the image and likeness of your habitual thought patterns.

—Joseph Murphy

Milly's first marriage ended on vacation in Yosemite National Park. Basking in the warm sunshine, the clean fresh air, and the breathtaking natural beauty, she turned to share the experience with her husband, who was on his cell phone to Venezuela, grunting and kicking the dirt, because he had just lost a huge business deal. The disconnection and loneliness was painful but familiar for her, so she worked harder and harder to make the relationship click.

Ten years after this incident, Milly and her second husband sat before me, with her marriage again on the rocks, partly for the same reasons. She felt that her husband was emotionally unavailable to her. Despite the fact that Milly had worked hard—perhaps too hard—to make this marriage work, her second husband wanted out. What was wrong with her that she couldn't keep a marriage together? Why did she keep marrying men who were emotionally disconnected?

Usually in these instances, the person is unconsciously choosing someone distant without consciously realizing it. After her second divorce and many hours of counseling, Milly realized that every romantic relationship she ever had was with an emotionally vacant man. The distance felt deeply familiar to her because it echoed the same loneliness she felt growing up with her absent, workaholic father who was uninvolved in her life. She had been trying all these years to fill that void with the only kinds of relationships she knew: more emotionally distant men.

Many times we vow to ourselves that we will avoid harmful situations, yet we end up in them anyway, fully knowing the consequences of our actions. Why do we continue to do things that we know will hurt us or cause us difficulties? An old adage defines insanity as repeating the same actions and expecting different results. Yet most of us are emotional repeaters. We keep getting involved in relationships that hurt us in the end. We go back to the same people for the same rejections. We keep trying to solve problems in the same old ways that in our hearts we already know don't work.

In order to change this pattern, the solution is to figure out what's not working and change it instead of repeating it. In other words, try to find new ways to solve old problems. Milly was able to see how repeating her bad choices kept her stuck. Emotionally distant men became a red flag for her. Now she is involved with a man who showers her with love and attention and with whom she shares emotional responsibility for their relationship.

Few things that happen to us are accidental. When we look closely at our choices, we can find the reasons behind our circumstances. Whether we want to admit it or not, we contribute to our life conditions each minute we take a breath. The key, of course, is to become more watchful and then take another course of action. My favorite poem is titled "An Autobiography in Five Short Chapters" by Portia Nelson (1980), which describes someone walking down a street and falling into a hole. A while later he walks down the street again and sees the hole but falls in it anyway. As time goes by he walks down the same street, sees the hole and walks around it. Eventually he walks down a different street and gets different results. The key here is to take a new course of action or a new approach to solving old problems. Stop using old ways that you already know don't work. Stop going back to the same people for the same rejections.

Are you a repeater in your personal life? If so, identify the things you keep doing that keep you unhappy. Then decide what new actions you can take that you haven't tried before. Taking those steps will move you to a different place that will bring you the satisfaction and joy you've been looking for and deserve.

Find Something Endearing About Someone Who Bugs You

The ego is the great fault finder. It presents the most subtle and insidious arguments for casting other people out of our hearts.

—Marianne Williamson

It was a long, hot summer in the South, and we were suffering through one of those sultry June mornings. Forecasts warned that temperatures would hit over 100 degrees. As I entered the office of my private practice, I discovered that Karen, my business partner, had turned off the air-conditioning the night before. Our offices are on the top floor of the building, and it felt like a steamy hot oven. Clients were sweating and fanning away the heat with waiting room magazines. At first I was upset, but then I reminded myself that her intentions were good, and the irritation evaporated. We had had a big discussion about cutting expenses and saving on utility costs, and I could see that she was trying really hard to do her part. Looking beyond my surface annoyance to her intentions endeared her to me.

I believe most people are doing the best they can most of the time. When we look beneath the surface of our disturbances and stretch to see the motives of people who bother us, it softens our reactions. A friend of mine was mad at her husband because he wanted her to keep the cell phone with her so he could reach her at all times during the day. She felt his request was unreasonable and felt controlled by it. But when she discussed the issue with him, he explained that it was his way of showing his love and concern for her. Seeing beneath the surface of her husband's actions and focusing on his motives melted her heart toward him.

I knew a supervisor once who went to great lengths to create defeat in his subordinates. The more inept they looked, the more competent he felt. He seemed more secure and in charge when things were falling apart or when an employee made a mistake. You could see the relief on his face when someone in the office made a mistake or hit a dead end. He would swell up like a frog and throw his weight around. But when someone handled a job well or figured out a computer problem that had stumped the rest of the office staff, the supervisor seemed to feel uncomfortable and agitated. Everyone with whom he worked despised this man who, driven by his own insecurities, used his superiority at the expense of others to disguise his own inferiority. But if you looked behind the "puffed up frog" you could see a scared little toad.

If you want to find more peace within yourself, here is one of the great paradoxes of life that can help you get there: develop an understanding that the people and situations that upset you the most have the most to offer you for your own growth. They can provide you with an opportunity to change yourself, if you're willing to try. Trying to see the wounds or the loving motivations of the people whose habits disturb you, you can soften how you feel and react.

Seeing people's faults as part of their human condition instead of seeing them as representing a "bad" person can help you cope in otherwise intolerable situations. And focusing on someone's intentions instead of their surface behaviors can make a big difference in how you respond to them. Think of someone you have condemned, criticized, or treated unkindly. Or someone whom you dislike, feel anger toward, or resent. Close your eyes and imagine yourself talking with that person. Look beyond his or her bothersome habits and try to imagine him or her as a wounded child. What kinds of hurtful experiences do you think might have led this person to become the way they are in order to cope? Are they overbearing because they were abused? Do they step on others so they can feel on top because they lack confidence in their own abilities? The next time you encounter this person, mentally "'fess up" to being annoyed (or whatever the routine feeling is), but be willing to see the person in a different light. When someone bugs you, find something about them that melts your heart. You'll feel more peaceful and loving toward the person, the situation, and yourself.

Do Something That Lets the Opposites in You Shine

It's what you learn after you know it all that counts.

—Judith Kelman

The extent of my acting experience had been playing a butterfly in the third grade. As Head Butterfly, it was my job to flutter around and wake up all the sleepy little flowers. Then at forty-three, I donned my powdered wig and hit the stage again, playing John Rugby in Shakespeare's *Merry Wives of Windsor*. I not only reawakened my acting abilities but also got to open up and show off another side of me. Dramatically speaking it was a small part—only three or four lines in three scenes. But in the drama of life it was my biggest role ever. The experience was a humbling one, to say the least. I played a servant who was beaten, pushed, pulled, kicked, and ordered around. I was a "slack" servant at that—someone who always tried to avoid work. No typecasting here. My character was the complete opposite from the true me, which was an overly structured workaholic and perfectionist who liked to be in control.

My need for order and predictability was challenged as the director cut my lines in some places and added lines in others. She changed scenes, putting me in some and taking me out of others. One night I thought, "Now, I hope things are finally set!" But I had put myself into a world that required fluidity. I was involved in a process where you try things out that might fit and see what works. Gradually, I learned to let go, do as I was told, and go with the flow. "Try things!" the director would say. "Play with your character."

At first I took my small role too seriously, as I did everything in life. I approached rehearsals like I had always approached my work—goal oriented and driven. This experience helped me embrace another more creative and relaxed part of myself. I discovered that living is not a series of projects to turn out like an assembly line and that the process can be meaningful and satisfying. I truly felt alive and whole, as if my life had shifted toward a more complete balance.

During our final bows, I felt sheer exhilaration. I had just accomplished one of the most important roles in life and neither the audience nor the cast knew the significance of this small part in my venture toward self-discovery.

Doing the same things day in and day out keeps us stuck on one track and prevents us from seeing and being all that we are. You can learn a lot by choosing an activity or hobby that gives you a chance to learn about the other "you's" that exist inside of yourself. Most of us are afraid of "the other side," even though there is no need to fear, because only wholeness and aliveness reside there.

You too can do something that will let your opposites shine. If you are rigid, you can do something that requires spontaneity and flexibility, as I did. If you are a perfectionist, choose a hobby, sport, or pastime and intentionally do it "imperfectly." If you are serious, logical, and systematic, engage in activities that stimulate the creative and intuitive side of your brain, such as art, dancing, or poetry. If you usually fly by the seat of your pants, you can do something that lets you feel the organized and accountable part of yourself. If you are too passive, you can experience what it's like to be forceful by taking an assertiveness class. If you are always on the go, you can do something that helps you stay put and feel calm (such as gardening, yoga, or just quiet contemplation). If most of your activities are sedentary, you can do something that gets you going (such as fast walking or aerobics). If your life is overly serious and intense, you can plan an activity that lets you feel your light-hearted and humorous side (such as going to a comedy club). And if your life feels unanchored, you can plan activities that put you in touch with your groundedness (such as balancing your checkbook or getting rid of clutter for an attic sale).

Human beings are multifaceted creatures. Most of us only let one side of ourselves show—usually the most comfortable side. Ask yourself which opposite parts of yourself you have held back and do something that gives your other side an equal voice.

3

Put Yourself In Harmony With Your Surroundings

You can hold back from the suffering of the world.
You have free permission to do so and it is in accordance
with your nature. But, perhaps this very holding back,
is the one suffering you could have avoided.

—Franz Kafka

Be a Harmony Freak Instead of a Control Freak

The world is not to be put in order, the world is order incarnate. It is for us to put ourselves in unison with this order.

—Henry Miller

The thought of putting myself in harmony with the natural order does not bring smiles to my face and warm fuzzies to my heart. In fact, this search for harmony represents some of the hardest challenges I've faced. One in particular occurred on September 22, 1989, when the eye of Hurricane Hugo struck my hometown of Charlotte, North Carolina. Ironically, I was stuck in Florida giving a luncheon address called "Don't Worry, Be Happy." The Charlotte International Airport closed because of runway damage, preventing me from getting home. Needless to say, this experience was the ultimate test for me.

So what do you do when you don't know what's happening to your loved ones and you can't protect them? I spoke with them by phone as the wind ravaged our city. Naturally, I was concerned about them, but I knew I was powerless to protect them from the deadly hurricane winds. Obviously, I could not change the course of Hugo, but I could change my thoughts about it. I implemented what I call the *harmony principle*, the essence of which is fitting yourself into any situation and rearranging your thoughts and feelings to accommodate to it.

Although worrying would be my natural inclination, rather than fret about, "How can this be happening? Why is this happening to me? What if they are all killed?" I had to accept the fact that "This *is* happening and I am powerless over the situation." I reminded myself that the universe has operated for millions of years without my worrying , controlling, or forcing my will to help it. So things would surely work out this time without my input. After letting go of my desire to *do* something, I realized that my loved ones were resourceful enough to take care of themselves—and they did. Fitting into the scheme of what was happening by accepting it and accepting my powerlessness actually gave me instant calm and hope.

Although natural disasters are not a frequent occurrence, you can apply the harmony principle in your everyday life when things don't go your way. After living on the planet for a while, most of us try to change things around so that they fit with what we want, as if we could change millions of years of harmony. We let the weather determine our moods rather than accepting it and going about our lives. We become annoyed with people who are late, forget appointments, bake bread differently, move slower, or have different beliefs and values than we do.

On a daily basis the need to control our lives can be an overpowering urge with which many of us struggle. Sometimes we find this need for control spills over into controlling other people and situations. Perhaps we tell our loved ones that if they would just do this or that, then everything would be okay. We try to stay on top of every situation at work. Or we become overly responsible in all areas of our lives. No wonder we're exhausted much of the time—we've been going *against* instead of *with* the grain. It's like trying to fit a square peg into a round hole or pushing the river in the opposite direction from which it naturally flows. Really, all you have to do is to think about how hard it is to change yourself. Then you will realize how difficult it is to change other people and situations. Some things cannot be changed, no matter what. No matter how hard we try, we cannot make the world and the people in it function the way we want them to.

The solution? The way out of this trap is to employ the harmony principle and surrender your control. You can let go of trying to control people and things that are beyond your control anyway. You can stop trying to make outcomes fit with what you think they "should be." You can step out from between other people and their problems, trusting them to find solutions. The first step is to stop wasting your time getting mad at things beyond your control, to start accepting them and accommodating your life to fit within them. You can surmount hardships by becoming harmonious with them—accepting them without complaints or resistance—and taking positive action wherever you can.

Accept Each Situation Exactly As It Is

If a man has nothing to eat, fasting is the most intelligent thing he can do.
—Hermann Hesse

Engines whining, the small airplane in which I was riding sounded as if it were slicing chunks out of the thick jungle fog as it cut its way through zero visibility. The tension inside the plane was as thick as the fog outside. Surrounded by majestic mountains of the Costa Rican rain forest, we were lost, without instruments and visibility. I sat directly behind the pilot, watching the sweat pouring down his neck as his head darted left and right in desperate attempts to see. Our hearts were in our throats for what seemed like an eternity, knowing we could collide with the side of a mountain in an instant. The pilot was swearing at air traffic control, who had okayed our earlier departure from the fog-shrouded jungle airport after an hour's delay. "Somebody's going to catch hell for this!" he swore. To make matters worse, the pilot had had two beers during our wait at the small terminal, which was really a jungle hut doubling as a local bar and landing strip.

Caught midair with no way to control the situation, there was nothing I could do. But there was actually a lot I could do. I could panic and yell and scream or surrender to my powerlessness over the situation. I closed my eyes, felt my own powerlessness and began meditating on the thought, "I'm letting go and letting God." I let all the tension evaporate from my body and made myself limp to accentuate the powerlessness. Calm enshrouded me. The pilot was able to backtrack and land at the same air strip from which we had departed.

There is an old saying that things change once we accept and love them *exactly* as they are, no matter how difficult, frustrating, and painful. Accepting circumstances that are beyond our control can bring us instant calm, because we can't do anything about them anyway. When we can accept each situation exactly as it is, instead of trying to make it the way we want it to be, our lives will run more smoothly. Every experience we have has a purpose in our lives, even though we may not understand it while it's happening.

The more we study the natural order of things and go with it, rather than resist it, the more we become harmonious with the world and find peace of mind. Many great teachings and spiritual practices say that peace of mind comes from going with the flow rather than from imposing our will by forcing, resisting, and clinging. One of the things I would recommend is that you take a personal inventory and ask yourself if there are things that you have been forcing, resisting, or clinging to in your life. One example would be *forcing* your way of doing something instead of accepting someone else's way equally as legitimate. I used to think that there was only one route to the mountains until I stopped forcing my rigid ways and started listening to the suggestions of others. Now I've learned that there are several routes which are faster and more scenic. Another example would be *resisting* someone else's point of view instead of stretching your mind and heart to see their side of the story. I used to be such a know-it-all, thinking I was always right and everybody else was wrong. Needless to say, that resistance caused me much heartache. A last example is *clinging* to old ways instead of letting go and moving on. For many of us that could be clinging to our youth instead of facing getting older or clutching an old relationship that is over and done with. After you have identified a pattern in your life, ask yourself what you can do differently that would put you more in harmony with your life.

When you find yourself trying to force situations into coming true, resisting situations over which you have no control, or clinging to things or people, try this simple exercise. Step back from the situation and look from the outside at what's going on. Ask yourself if your will is overpowering you and try to let it go. Obviously the universe has something else in store for you. Consider other courses of action that are less complicated and that flow more naturally and let instant calm and happiness flow into your life.

Live with Less and Have More

Happiness is produced not so much by great pieces of good fortune that seldom happen as by little advantages that occur every day.

—Benjamin Franklin

The colors of orange and magenta swirled through my house as ten Tibetan Buddhist monks entered it for a five-day stay. I had the honor of hosting the monks, who were in town for a week of concerts, chanting, healing prayers and constructing sand mandalas, in what was being touted as "The Joyful Wisdom Tour." My experience of housing the monks taught me many lessons, the most important of which was "keep things simple."

My friends and loved ones and I so wanted to support their cause that we approached the anticipated moment in deeply imbedded Western style by overcooking, overscheduling, and overdoing for the monks. While they were gracious and grateful, the leader gently asked for "not too much." Exiled by Communist China from their native land with no means of support, these men needed very little to be happy. Always smiling and laughing and emphasizing compassion and love for everyone was the simple practice that sustained them. They had no desire or need for extravagance or complicated Western lifestyles.

Many Eastern spiritual practices teach that things in their original simplicity contain their own natural power, power that is spoiled or lost when that simplicity is changed. The clutter and complications of the material world can interfere with our happiness. A simpler approach cuts through the complexities of our everyday lives. Using the simple tools that we are given keeps our path clear of clutter. In the words of Henry David Thoreau, "Our life is frittered away by detail . . . simplify, simplify."

Many of us believe we need elaborate experiences outside ourselves to entertain us and provide us with the excitement of life: compact discs, DVD players, computers, cell phones, and endless other gadgets. The need for this stimulation often leads to excess. Sometimes we go to great lengths to seek thrills by traveling to distant places, spending lots of money, and taking financial risks. An old Chinese proverb says, "To pretend to satisfy one's desires by possession is like using straw to put out a fire." Our lives become jumbled with acquiring material possessions and achieving outward success and importance. The more we try to analyze and rationalize our lives, the more complicated and crowded they become. We turn our problems over and over in our minds and worry. They grow bigger than they actually are. A simple approach cuts through the static and noise these complications can bring.

The message? Less is more. Richness and abundance are contained in simplicity, because streamlining our lives can help us find peace and happiness. The free, easy, and simple things in life are what bring us the most satisfaction, and the complex, expensive things can lead us away from it. We don't have to look far and wide for abundance, because we already have it right under our noses, in the uncomplicated acts of cooking, planting a garden, stroking a pet, caressing a baby, taking a walk, or having heart-to-heart talks with loved ones. All we need to do is acknowledge what is already in front of us.

When your personal life is jumbled with material things, unwanted or unhealthy relationships, and too many appointments and commitments, you can ask yourself what needs eliminating, downsizing, or simplifying. Then take the steps to make this change. Instead of taking on more commitments, ask yourself what obligations or chores you can eliminate from your to-do list. Instead of purchasing more things, ask yourself what you can sell or give away. Every time you consume or do less, you're investing more in you. You will discover that simplifying and quieting your life with *less* can translate into *more* clarity, happiness, and peace of mind.

Release Your Emotional Poisons

Nothing on earth consumes a man more quickly than the passion of resentment.

—Friedrich Wilhelm Nietzsche

I was at the lowest point of my life, and I didn't care if I lived or died. I had just ended a long-term relationship with someone I thought was my soul mate. The love of my life had found someone else. I was numb—as if recovering from surgery after having part of my soul removed. It felt like half of *me* was gone. I was angry, hurt, and emotionally exhausted. I couldn't eat or sleep and nothing mattered to me anymore.

My friend, Robert, convinced me to take a week in the Caribbean to get away from the pain. So we hopped a plane to Jamaica, thinking I'd escape the unpleasant thoughts and feelings and perhaps it would cheer me up (sound familiar? It's called "geographic escape"). Of course, the resentment that consumed me accompanied us on the trip, hovering over me and reminding me of how I'd been betrayed. All I could think about was getting even with the third person who came between me and my beloved. Replaying the images and scenes in my mind was like dumping the poison of resentment into my system. The obsessive thoughts created rage, insomnia, and loss of appetite. I'd lay awake until the wee morning hours plotting my revenge—like that little boy in me who used to write fun adventure stories. Only this time, it was real stuff and the storyline had become mean, spiteful, and ugly. My need for revenge unearthed a deep need within me to express my inner pain in an outside way. Now that I look back, those negative obsessive thoughts and emotional poisons that I created in my head stayed there, hurting no one else but me.

I attribute my own healing from this emotional poison to the *release principle*, which stresses the importance of getting rid of what you don't want in your life in order to make room for better to enter. It began in the course of my Jamaican trip as I lay on the beach. I gradually had gotten fed up with feeling so miserable, so I decided to try and let some of the pain go. Laying in the sun, I visualized all the hostility that I had been carrying around suddenly evaporating from my body, like steam off a hot street after a summer rain. As I pictured the thoughts and feelings leaving my body, I began to actually feel lighter and less burdened. I opened my eyes and a Jamaican man shimmied up a coconut palm tree, cracked open a coconut, and offered me half to drink. Asking nothing in return, he smiled and walked away.

As I repeated this simple release meditation in the months to come, good continued to flow into my life. The nightmares subsided, my appetite returned, and I felt an inner calm that helped me sleep like a baby. I began to think more positively about myself and the old relationship, wishing harm to no one. During those months a cornucopia of positive events poured into my life. I received more money than ever before and during the following year, I established a healthier relationship with the same person whom I thought I had lost. We are still together after thirty years, and both of us look back on that experience as a blessing that taught us more about who we are and that added a richness and strength that binds us closer together today.

I am convinced that these dramatic changes resulted from the release of resentment, which cleared a space in my mind and heart for me to receive life's gifts. This experience also convinced me that meditation and contemplation are the keys to personal happiness.

What grudges or resentments do you need to release so that you can create the space for greater peace and happiness? Think of any person (including yourself) toward whom you harbor negative thoughts or feelings, whom you have condemned, criticized, or treated unkindly. Think of someone whom you dislike, feel anger toward, resent, or in some way feel out of harmony with. Picture the resentment in your mind and heart and be ready to let the feelings go for *your* sake. Repeat the following release exercise as often as you need to and picture the self-destructive thoughts and feelings slowly evaporating from your mind: *I release, one by one, all the thoughts and feelings of resentment that I have carried and that have weighed heavily on my mind and heart. I wish you no harm. I bury the hatchet once and for all and set myself free. In this empty space I am open to receiving life's blessings.*

Use the "F" Word in Difficult Situations

Flow with whatever may happen and let your mind be free: Stay centered by accepting whatever you are doing. This is the ultimate.

—Chuang Tzu

"Flow." What a great "F" word! The ability to bend and sway with whatever life sends our way. The ability to fit ourselves into any unexpected situation instead of trying to force the situation to fit our specifications. Flow has been one of the hardest things for me to incorporate into my life. By now, you probably know why. Remember my experience at the retreat center? It was a mirror for me to see my strong need for control and my resistance to flow, one of the biggest lessons I'm still trying to learn. The author Cherie Carter-Scott (1998) summed me up in a nutshell: "If resistance has been a theme throughout your life, then surrender will appear in your curriculum."

One incident in particular stands out in my mind: I flew to New York to tape a segment for the television show *20/20*, arriving at La Guardia Airport in the midst of a cab strike. The city had hired cab drivers from the outer perimeter to transfer passengers from the airport to their hotels. My companion, Sylvia, and I ended up being driven by a charming Pakistani man who was unfamiliar with the city. I gave him the same hotel name the producer had given me: The Mayflower. He threw both palms faceup to say he didn't know the directions to the hotel. By the time we hit Madison Avenue he had asked three other cab drivers, none of whom knew the whereabouts of the Mayflower Hotel. Assuming the mistake had been all mine, I checked the producer's letter to verify the hotel's name. Sure enough, I was shocked and embarrassed to read "Mayfair," not "Mayflower." After apologizing profusely, yet feeling relieved to know my error, I felt now the driver could get us to our destination. Again, both palms darted skyward, a gesture that caused me to feel frustrated and annoyed. Here we had spent forty-five minutes on a wild goose chase around New York City. Again the cab driver stopped a fellow driver asking directions to the Mayfair.

He turned to me and informed me that there are two Mayfair hotels and asked me which one I wanted. I hadn't a clue, but instinctively chose the one on Central Park West. He drove to Columbus Circle and pulled to the curb. Lost, he shrugged his shoulders and punctuated the air with his palms. In desperation, I leaned out the window and yelled to anyone in the city who would listen, "Does anybody know how to get to the Mayfair Hotel?" A pedestrian on the corner pointed and instructed us that it was right around the block. As we rounded the corner, we were perplexed to see the *Mayflower* Hotel looming before our eyes. By now we felt like we had entered the Twilight Zone. But indeed our room was at the Mayflower all along. The producer had verbally said "Mayflower" but accidentally written "Mayfair." We were being guided in the right destination all along even though we felt lost and confused. Even the pedestrian on the street directed us to the Mayflower, even though I had asked for the Mayfair.

The moral to this story: Sometimes in our lives when we think we're lost or not in control, flowing helps things turn out okay in the end. Instead of letting resistance stunt our growth, we can open ourselves to the lessons that life teaches us. Life is like a river flowing to the sea, and we don't even have to swim. All we have to do is relax and flow with it. Surrendering our resistance allows us to go with the flow. We can trust that we're being led by a force greater than ourselves. Flowing with that faith can get us through difficult times without the oppositional reactions of resistance, frustration, and rage.

See if you can identify one person or event that challenges your ability to flow. The next time you're in the presence of this person or event, try to let go of your resistance and simply flow. Notice how much freer you feel. Notice how flowing helps reduce your anxiety. And notice how practicing the "F" words of fluidity, flexibility, and flowing brings you more happiness and peace of mind over the long haul.

Grasp at the Great Shadows in Your Life

We are afraid to let go of our petty reality in order to grasp at a great shadow.

—Antoine de Saint Exupery

I used to live my life by the book. So naturally when a friend asked me to go to a yoga meditation center, I declined. I figured it was some kind of cult where they'd make me drink Kool-Aid. Besides, after my first experience at a spiritual retreat center, I'd had my fill of "that stuff," which I'd decided was more trouble than it was worth. No, I would lead my life by the straight and narrow, thank you very much. Still, something within me said, "What the heck? You don't have anything better to do and, if nothing else, you can have a good laugh."

So I ended up going. And it was heartrending. I was profoundly moved by the speaker who gave many sound ideas of how to live our lives with contentment and happiness. There really was something to "that stuff" after all. I was so thankful my rigid standards lapsed long enough for me to change my life. As a result of my own positive experience, I introduced two or three of my friends to the meditation center, and they shared with their friends, and so on. The ripple effect led to countless others discovering these teachings. Even this book came about partly from that experience. I could name three or four other examples of how breaking with my petty reality and grasping at a "great shadow" has been life changing: lucrative investments, rich friendships, adventure, and fun-loving times.

Rules, routines, and schedules. We need them to keep our lives orderly, but how many wonderful experiences and people have we excluded by living our lives by the book? If we examine the way we live carefully, we would see how we limit ourselves through rigidity. Perhaps this is done unintentionally out of a need for security—but it's still limiting. We frequent the same restaurants, hold the same job, follow the same daily routines, and stay in the same close-knit circle of friends. Holding on to the same ruts, routines, and routes may be familiar and comfortable, but it also limits the scope of our happiness. Maybe we are reluctant to do things differently, because the old ways are easier and there's always the hope that maybe this time things will work. Or the unfamiliarity of the new and different ways and ideas may be threatening, even though they might be the key to making the changes we need to make.

I am reminded of the ancient tale about Nasrudin, who lost his house key on the way home one night. A stranger passed by and found Nasrudin down on all fours under a streetlight searching frantically for his key. Perplexed, the stranger asked Nasrudin why he was on his hands and knees. And when Nasrudin told him his dilemma, the stranger, being a kind man, bent down to help him search for the key. After three hours of futile searching, the stranger asked, "Are you sure you dropped the key in this spot?" Nasrudin said, "Oh, no!" Pointing toward a small alley, he explained, "I dropped it over there in the dark." Frustrated and angry, the stranger exploded, "Then why are you looking for it here under the lamppost?" Nasrudin replied, "Because the light's better here."

The solutions to all our problems are in the shadows. And into the darkness, where we've never been, is where we must go to solve them. Although the human mind prefers sameness and resists change, change is the one thing in life you can count on. Clinging to the familiar and comfortable puts us at odds with the natural flow of life. No matter how hard we clutch the old ways, change will drag us, kicking and screaming, into doing things differently.

One important approach is to deliberately eliminate sameness and welcome change in some area of your life. Eliminate the boredom and roadblocks to your happiness that sameness creates. Welcome opposing views, knowing that everyone's way of thinking is different from yours but valid nonetheless. Getting out of your rut can start as simply as changing your daily routine, like taking a different route home from work. If you've been unsuccessful at relationships, take a different approach. Choose just one thing to do differently, no matter how small, that you have never done before; then stand back and watch your life bloom.

Create Harmony By Listening to Your Inner Guides

████████████████████

One man gets nothing but discord out of a piano; another gets harmony. No one claims the piano is at fault. Life is about the same. The discord is there, and the harmony is there. Study to play it correctly, and it will give forth the beauty; play it falsely, and it will give forth the ugliness. Life is not at fault.

—Ninon de L'Enclos

On some mornings as I drive to work, I ask myself, "Who's driving today?" or "Who's in charge of my life at this moment?" Wait! Don't throw this book in the trash yet. I haven't lost my mind. It's just that I believe that all of us are multifaceted human beings, and that we contain many inner guides or different parts of ourselves—each with their own positive and negative character. Don't get me wrong: I'm not talking about multiple personalities. But there are many sides to both you and me. Let me explain.

Sometimes my *wise man* is leading my life, making smart business investments and guiding me with a steady hand through serious personal and professional decisions. But most of the time my *hero* monopolizes my life. That's the disciplined and motivated part of me with high standards and a commitment to make the world a better place. My hero's downside has been the overresponsible and hard-driving perfectionism that runs rough-shod over anything that gets in the way of my goals—relationships, health, relaxation, being in the present. My hero can become so fixated on the goal that he can be insensitive to others' feelings. When I'm aware that this is happening, I activate yet another part of me that I call the *softie*. This is my sensitive, caring, and compassionate side that is considerate of others, loving them and putting them first. Then there's the *wizard*, who helps me stop and smell the roses, pay attention to the process in life, and see the magic contained there.

60

He helps me transform character flaws into strengths and to keep my eye on the present moment as I move toward my goals.

But my all-time favorite part of myself is the *clown*, the funny, carefree, and light-hearted side with a zest for life and not a care in the world. He is the playful side that restores the lost joy and freedom I sometimes forfeit when my hero insists on the seriousness of staying on track. He is also the inner guide who shows up the least, usually on vacations and weekends when I'm not burdened with the slings and arrows of life in the fast lane. My clown keeps my hero in check. He is the guide that I long for and try to involve more often in my life—the part that fills me with joy and makes me feel good.

You too have a set of inner guides that may be similar or totally different from mine. The ways in which we see our lives and behave in the world are defined by which inner guide currently dominates our thoughts and actions. The wizard can help you create a new way of living that is fulfilling and magical, the wise man or wise woman assures that your decisions are sound and beneficial, the clown keeps things light and enjoyable, the softie helps you remain sensitive to the feelings of those around you, and the hero can help you successfully reach your goals.

Periodically, I have found it helpful to evaluate my life and ask myself which of these inner guides are active and which are silent in my life. I also consider which ones I can activate this week to bring my life into greater harmony. I think you too will find this exercise helpful if you try it for a few days. Try standing back and looking at yourself. See how many different sides to yourself you can identify. Give each guide a name, a costume, and a character all its own. Note which ones you like the most and which ones you like the least.

Each morning as you wrap your hands around the steering wheel of your car or the railing of the train, ask yourself who's center stage today. Which guide has dominated your actions and which ones are asleep? And most importantly, which guides do you need to activate to check the ones you don't like in order to bring more calm, happiness, and harmony into your life?

Wait Without Clicking Your Nails

*Most people don't care where they're going as long as they're in
something that gets them there in a hurry.*

—Andy Rooney

A woman in North Carolina has angrily left carts full of groceries at supermarkets because the checkout lines were too long. Although she knows she'll just have to shop again later, if the line is too long, she won't wait.

A salesman in Atlanta times to the minute the trip from his house to the airport so he doesn't have to wait. He leaves his house an hour before flight time. It takes thirty to forty-five minutes for him to get to the airport and ten to fifteen minutes to park his car and check his bags. With this system he can walk up and be the last person on board because he "hates sitting and waiting for things." Instead of leaving a little earlier so he doesn't have to hurry, he says there are too many other things he has to do.

Now let's be honest here: Do you have stories like the ones above because you hate to wait? Well, join the Waiting Haters Club, a popular group that's growing every day. Waiting is probably one of the most challenging things facing most of us today, yet one of the most necessary to learn. I remember in the 1960s we foretold that by the millennium our technology would free us for more relaxation and leisure time and that four-day work-weeks would be the norm. Instead, just the opposite has happened. From California to the Carolinas things are moving faster, and people are working everywhere—at home, on planes, in restaurants, and even in the Amazon jungle—day and night, seven days a week.

"Fast Food" flashes in red neon; "Quick Copying," boasts the e-mail ad; "Speedy Service," reads the restaurant advertisement. The signs of our times reflect our hurried and harried lifestyles. Haunted by a constant sense of time urgency, we try to do two or three things at once. We're so accustomed to speeding from task to task that waiting conflicts with our constantly revving engines. We expect people and situations to match our hurried pace, and we become annoyed if we're kept waiting. Waiting lists and waiting rooms are not our cup of tea, and we want the cashier to move the lines through quicker and the physician to see us immediately upon our arrival.

In the 1970s, before computers, I completed my dissertation on a typewriter, using white-out to correct mistakes. At the time it didn't feel slow to me because that was all we had. Today I see people pounding fists and clicking nails on desktops because their computers don't move fast enough. Our cars are the fastest in history, yet we've all seen (or been) the five o'clock commuter who pounds fists and clicks nails on the steering wheel in frustration. How much faster do we have to go to be satisfied?

As our lives move faster and faster, waiting will become more common yet more difficult, because of constantly increasing expectations that force us to hurry—even if we don't really have to. My advice is that waiting is here, so we need to get used to it. One thing you can do is experiment with the waiting game by waiting when you don't necessarily have to. You can start by trying it on your own terms, perhaps on a day off or when you have spare time. Schedule a doctor's appointment (you almost always have to wait there), deliberately put yourself in the longest grocery line, or drive in morning or afternoon traffic—all to practice waiting. Caught in rush-hour traffic or a slow-moving line? Seize the waiting moments as times for personal reflection and replenishment. Take deep breaths, tell yourself you're *choosing* to wait. Instead of getting annoyed at people who move at a snail's pace, try to see them as an example of how to slow down. Use the extra time to people-watch and perhaps you'll see a mirror of your own impatience and irritability. Immerse yourself in the process of waiting, lingering, and killing time.

Waiting can have its advantages. It can even be an antidote to stress, if you're willing to see it that way. Learning to wait can be like cushioning your life with shock absorbers. It provides you space in your day to stretch and breathe so that you can take a more human pace and pay more attention to the present. It prepares you to open your heart and to receive whatever life brings you at the moment. Waiting can be a way of putting yourself in harmony with the present. So the next time you are forced to wait, use it to your advantage and *choose* to wait. In the long run you will learn to kill time instead of letting it kill you.

4

Be Willing to Change

We must all obey the great law of change.
It is the most powerful law of nature.

—Edmund Burke

Learn Your Lessons Well

It ain't no disgrace for a man to fall, but to lie there and grunt is.

—Josh Billings

Once upon a time Nasrudin and his master went hunting in the forest. The master cut his thumb while shooting his bow and arrow because he held it incorrectly. Nasrudin stopped the bleeding and bandaged the deep wound as his master moaned in pain. In an attempt to console his master, Nasrudin said, "Sir, there are no mistakes, only lessons, and we can learn from them if we're willing."

The master became enraged. "How dare you lecture me!" he barked.

And with that he threw Nasrudin into a deserted well and continued on without his devoted servant.

A little further on, a group of forest people captured the master and took him to their chief for human sacrifice. The fire was roasting hot, and the master was about to be thrown into it when the chief noticed his bandaged thumb and set him free. It was a rule that all sacrificial victims had to be perfect specimens. Realizing how right Nasrudin had been, the master rushed back to the well to rescue his faithful servant. Acknowledging his unjust actions, the master pulled Nasrudin out and asked him to forgive him for the terrible mistake.

Nasrudin assured him that he had not made a mistake at all. On the contrary, he insisted that there was another lesson concealed here. Nasrudin told his master that he had done Nasrudin a great service by throwing him into the well. He thanked his master for saving his life explaining that if he had continued with him into the forest, the forest people would have taken him for sacrifice and surely he would had died.

"You see," Nasrudin ventured, "there are no mistakes, only lessons to learn. What we call our mistakes can be blessings in disguise, if we're willing to learn from them."

This time the master smiled and nodded in agreement.

Lessons are necessary to achieve success. In fact, success is built on lessons, which are built on failing. The toddler cannot learn to walk without falling down. The older child cannot learn to ride a bicycle without falling off on the first few tries. You cannot climb the success ladder without missing an occasional rung. It's a package deal: success and failure go together like a hand and glove, Adam and Eve, Abbott and Costello, or cookies and milk.

Life is full of ups and downs, and there will be times when you might forget, make a error, or say or do the wrong thing. But no matter how serious the gaff, you don't have to sink into self-pity. You can get up, brush yourself off, and keep on going. The key is to reframe your mistakes as lessons and figure out what you can learn about yourself from them. This frame of mind makes your lessons valuable opportunities that are essential for your personal and career success. Not only do they make you wise, they are the building blocks that make you successful. Thinking of mistakes and failure as lessons can keep you in a positive frame and keep you from feeling discouraged and hopeless. Mistakes viewed as lessons are supportive and build success; mistakes viewed as failures are destructive and undermine success. Lessons are proactive ways of taking what comes your way and making it work to your advantage. Turning mistakes into lessons is another way to build yourself up instead of tear yourself down—by simply reframing your life conditions.

Here I offer you perhaps the biggest challenge in this book (at least it is for me). Try to look upon the people who upset you as messengers or teachers who are there to help you learn more about yourself. Just as the master was doing a great service to Nasrudin by throwing him in the well, the people you think are your enemies may be your best friends. Those who anger you, embarrass you, hurt you, contradict you, and yes, even betray you are doing you a great favor. They are bringing you lessons that make you wiser, stronger, and better able to successfully meet the next challenge that comes your way.

Stop Using Others as Target Practice When You're "Dead Wrong"

Feeling right is a strong drug. Some people sacrifice a lot to be right. Ever hear the expression 'dead right'?

—John Roger and
Peter McWilliams

I will always remember the day I jumped down the librarian's throat about a book that had been checked out by another faculty member for two months. On my third trip to the library just to get this book, I was furious when I was told it was still unavailable. I demanded that the librarian search the computer and tell me the person's name so I could talk with him or her. She searched and gave me a disconcerting look.

"We're not supposed to give out that information, but in this case I think it's okay," she said.

"Well?" I demanded impatiently.

"It says *you're* the faculty member who has the book, sir."

Needless to say, I was flabbergasted, but I held on to my anger. I stormed out of the library in a huff and raced home to vindicate myself. After ransacking my office to find the book, I finally discovered it in a huge stack of other books. The next time I was in the library I made sure to offer my sheepish apologies to the librarian.

How many times have we refused to admit we were wrong and unleashed our hostility and frustrations on innocent bystanders? When things don't go the way we want, we can first look within ourselves for the reason. We can ask ourselves how we created the problems we face and how we can resolve them responsibly without finding a scapegoat. Facing the outcomes of our own actions takes us from emotional adolescence to emotional maturity.

The embarrassing situation with the librarian taught me a lesson: I am not always right, and it's unfair to blame others for my own shortcomings. Unfortunately, we live in a society in which people blame something or someone else for their wrong actions a good bit of the time. Just look at the news: A woman spills hot coffee on herself and blames the restaurant; a man gets caught in a bad storm at sea and blames the Weather Channel; a young man randomly assassinates several people and blames his psychiatrist.

Let's face it: It's difficult, sometimes even humiliating, to admit it when we're wrong—even when we know it. Some people have such fragile egos that they'd go to their graves just to be right. Some people fear others will not respect them if they fail to be perfect, so they exaggerate their successes and hide their shortcomings. They brag about a huge raise but hide the fact that they were raked over the coals because of an oversight in their sales report. They announce their acceptance at Yale, but say nothing of their rejection at Harvard. They celebrate winning two hundred dollars in Vegas but hide the fact that they lost five hundred dollars the same day. But our strength, and our happiness come from the realization that we can say, "I was wrong" or "I made a mistake," and still survive. There is weakness in covering our tracks and strength in openly admitting our mistakes.

Feeling that you constantly have to fight to prove your point can take a lot out of a person. Always being right is a huge burden to carry—one that's impossible to maintain for long. I must admit I've gotten better. Now I ask myself if it's really worth the emotional and physical toll to always be right in petty disagreements. I know from experience that once we stop blaming and start taking responsibility for our wrongdoing, our lives start to improve. It takes a strong ego and a self-confident person to let someone else be right for a change. But the more you practice, the easier it gets. And by letting go of the need to be right, you can diffuse tension, restore peace, and help you feel better about yourself.

Try this exercise. The next time you are in a tug-of-war over who's right and who's wrong, simply ask yourself whether you'd rather be right or happy. If your answer is "happy," then remind yourself that being right is a burden that you no longer want or need to carry. This thought can emancipate you from feeling that you always must be right. When you're wrong, promptly admitting it will free you, diffuse the situation, earn the respect of others, and leave you at peace with yourself.

Walk a Mile in Someone's Shoes

The body travels more easily than the mind, and until we have limbered up our imagination we continue to think as though we had stayed home. We have not really budged a step until we take up residence in someone else's point of view.

—John Erskine

Imagine having dinner in an expensive restaurant with someone special. You've looked forward to a quiet evening of candlelight, soft music, and intimate conversation. Your server, however, is invasive, impatient, and short tempered. How would you feel? Most people would say annoyed or angry, and perhaps rightly so. Now imagine that a friend who's eating at the restaurant knows the server, comes over to inform you that the server's son was killed in an automobile wreck the previous day, but she had to work anyway because she's broke.

Now how would you feel? Most people would say sad, sorry, or empathetic. What happened? How can your emotions switch from anger one second to compassion in the next? The server hasn't changed. She's still being her irritating self. So what changed? You did. The way you were looking at the situation changed, and because you have more information, you see more of who the server is than you did at first.

Empathy neutralizes anger. The ability to put yourself in someone else's shoes and see their point of view is a powerful technique to help you deal with disgruntled people. Deliberately putting yourself in someone else's place and feeling what it's like to be them can increase your understanding and sensitivity. It can liberate you from narrow and negative thinking and help you to be less quick to judge. Using this technique can help you respond to situations in human ways you can feel good about. It also can help you become more patient and loving, experiencing difficult people and situations with less frustration and with more peace of mind.

You can use this technique with friends and loved ones to help settle disputes or to help you keep calm when someone else is exploding. Suppose you've had an enjoyable day of serenity and relaxation when all of a sudden your loved one comes bounding in the door, cursing, slamming doors, and kicking the dog. Most likely you would resent the fact that he or she is raining all over your parade. You might even start slamming things and cursing yourself. But if you take the time to go beneath the surface and find out the cause of the huff, you're more likely to neutralize your anger and respond with compassion and empathy. Suppose, for example, your loved one was fired, had a wreck, or was just diagnosed with a terminal illness. Whatever the root cause of the unsettling behavior, taking the time to discover it before you react can keep your mind from stunting your growth, helping you become more the kind of person you want to be.

Now you might be thinking, "But why should I be empathetic to someone who's blasting me—loved one or stranger? That just doesn't make sense!" First of all, using empathy rather than anger as a first response can make you a more loving, kind, and compassionate person. And if that's not a good enough reason, there are several other reasons why this approach works in your best interests. Being empathetic allows you to maintain control over a situation, keeping your cool and integrity intact. It also enables you to see the full situation from more than just your standpoint and to respond in a way that facilitates good communication. In professional situations, taking the higher ground of understanding with a client or coworker with a gripe actually can give you the upper hand and can diffuse the volatility of a potentially negative situation.

Think of just one person you can empathize with today, someone who has done something to upset you, and temporarily suspend your point of view (you don't have to give it up for good). Try to imagine walking around inside that person's body and experiencing the upsetting event in their skin, through their eyes, and with their heart. Then notice your anger dissipate. You feel in charge of yourself. It's a very contented, self-satisfying state, and you can't wait for the next opportunity to do it again, because it feels good!

Practice Forgiveness for Your Own Sake, If Not for Others

To err is human, to forgive, divine

—Alexander Pope

A friend of mine invited her best friend to come live with her and her husband and their two children. During the course of the next year my friend kept house, did all the cooking, and remained a good mother and wife. She was delighted that her girlfriend could become part of her family. But the generous offer turned sour when my friend discovered that her girlfriend had been sleeping with her husband for several months. Her husband and best friend moved away together and were eventually married, leaving my friend in a cloud of hurt and betrayal. She was left with an emptiness that quickly filled with bitterness, resentment, anger, and hatred for two people who had been her closest allies.

Holding on to those negative feelings for the next three years actually caused my friend more pain and hurt than the two people who hurt her. The husband and girlfriend had begun a happy new life in another city and weren't affected at all by the rage my friend had been storing. But my friend suffered the emotional and physical consequences of carrying those stored feelings for years. She couldn't have her husband, but she *could* have her anger and bitterness toward him. If she gave that up too, she would have lost everything. Her bitterness and resentment at least gave her something to hold on to.

Perhaps you think that holding on to resentments will give you emotional retaliation that feels good. Giving up your grudges and resentments, you fear, would unleash a groundswell of emotions like a bursting dam. Or your biggest fear might be that there would be nothing left for you to hold on to. The truth is that you do yourself more harm than good by holding grudges. It keeps the hurtful situation at the center of your daily experience and keeps you emotionally imprisoned by it. There is an old saying that those who anger you, conquer you. Holding grudges also takes a lot of emotional energy that gets displaced onto other people as anger—energy that you could use in more positive ways that would bring you greater benefits.

"Why should your friend forgive her husband and best friend?" you may explode. "That was an unforgivable thing they did to her!" To that I answer yes, it was a hurtful and painful incident. But nothing is unforgivable. You don't have to condone what the husband and friend did, but they did nothing "to her." It was her reaction that harmed her. This is one of those hardships I've been talking about throughout this book that can strengthen us—a condition that causes us to question, "Is this good luck or bad luck?" It's up to my friend to decide for herself whether she will be *harmed* or *helped* by the incident. No one else can make that decision for her.

You, too, can make a conscious decision to forgive someone toward whom you have harbored negative thoughts and feelings that you'd like to release for your own sake. But a word of caution about forgiveness before you commit to it. Don't forgive someone if your heart is not in it or if you feel the need to make a conspicuous display of martyrdom by forgiving the accused in a grandstand fashion. The writer Sidney Harris once said, "There's no point in burying a hatchet if you're going to put up a marker on the site." You have to be honestly ready and willing to let go of the anger, hurt, and self-pity before you make the commitment to do it.

Ask yourself if you are ready to forgive the person *entirely* and *completely*. Are you ready to forgive this person even for things he or she has yet to do or will continue to do? Remember that you must be willing to forgive that person *totally* for all past, present, and future behaviors. Once you can truthfully answer yes, write down on a sheet of paper this person's name and what he or she did or does that arouses your strong feelings. Close your eyes and imagine yourself talking with the person. Visualize him or her doing whatever it is that bothers you. Next, see yourself forgiving that person *completely*. After you feel true forgiveness in your heart, open your eyes, tear the paper into tiny pieces, and throw it into the trash bin. The next time you think negative thoughts toward this person, remind yourself that you've already consigned those feelings to the trash.

Don't Be a Worry Wart

Worry does not empty tomorrow of its sorrow; it empties today of its strength.

—Corrie Ten Boom

In my early twenties I had great difficulty with weekends and holidays when there was too much free time. Waking up on a morning with nothing to do left me with a feeling of foreboding. I felt fidgety during those idle hours. I felt that, if I let my guard down, I would surely be hit by all the bad things I worried about in my quiet hours. So I coped with worry by staying on guard for the unexpected, even when everything was okay. I packed my weekends full and overscheduled my life so that it would feel more predictable, so I'd know exactly what would happen next and how to prepare for it. Although staying busy seemed to alleviate worry, it robbed me of flexibility, spontaneity, relaxing moments, play, and just plain enjoyment of life. And I was tense much of the time.

Worry is one of those cruel ghosts that can haunt you day and night. Can you still perform on the job? Are you still lovable? Is your youth fading? Worry goes ahead of you like a scouting party before you face challenging situations. It stalks you when you have a big day on the job and lurks over your shoulder when you're trying to make important relationships work. It's a constant reminder that you don't have forever to complete your tasks on this planet. The anchor of worry can weigh you down and bring you to your knees when you cart around all your problems from the past, from the present, and those that you expect to have in the future. Such worry does not erode tomorrow's problems; it erodes your strength to deal with them today.

Sometimes the biggest worries occur when everything is going well, and you tell yourself that things are just too good to be true. Instead of embracing the calm, your mind braces for the worst. When you are worried during both calm times *and* troubled times, you create a worried, fearful life twenty-four hours a day, seven days a week. Living this way, you can never have the portion of happy times that you're entitled to. Most of your worries never happen, but you lose endless hours being upset when you could be enjoying life. Worry weakens you physically, too. It keeps you in the fight or flight mode—a state of emergency in which your body secretes adrenaline. Constant worry creates wear and tear on your body, just as if you actually went through the dreaded experience. The consequence is emotional exhaustion, burnout, and physical ailments.

Are you waiting for the ax to fall or worrying that something bad might happen to you, even though there is no good reason for it? Why waste your life worrying it away when worry is a habit you can change? When you feel gloom and doom for no good reason, start with realizing that catastrophic thinking is nothing but a thought in your mind—a synapse firing in your brain. It has nothing to do with what will *actually* happen. Besides, you are worrying about things you can't control anyway.

If you make a conscious effort to live in the present, your actions will be more productive than worrying about situations beyond your control. Meditation is a strategy that helps train you to live in the moment, and quiets your mind and body. When you meditate, your heart rate and brain-wave patterns slow down, the immune system gets a boost, and body chemistry secretes life-sustaining hormones.

Try this meditation for just three minutes before leaving for work or before drifting off to sleep. In a quiet and comfortable place—your office, car, or a cozy place at home—close your eyes and clear your mind of cluttered thoughts. Then call up the biggest worries swirling in your head. See yourself letting go of each worry one by one. Then visualize a shower of raindrops—each one a pellet of calm—gently falling and cleansing your mind of fear. Imagine the empty space in your mind being filled with these peaceful, calming images and thoughts. Later, when the worries compete for your attention, remind yourself that they are gone. Continue this meditation as often as necessary to evacuate your worries and restore peace of mind.

Start each day fresh, free of the residue of worry. You'll be surprised at how much better your life will be when you start clean and live in the now by leaving the past and future where they belong and expecting the best life has to offer. In the words of Wayne Dyer, "Now is all we have. Everything that has ever happened to you and anything that is ever going to happen to you, is just a thought."

Have Patience in Reaching Your Goals

████████████████████████████

It is the law of all progress that it is made by passing through some stages of inability—and that it may take a very long time.

—Pierre Teilhard de Chardin

One thing I've noticed about myself is that when I have a goal, I'm impatient to get there without delay. Whether it's taking a trip, writing a book, saving extra money, losing weight, or moving forward on my spiritual path, I would prefer to skip the intermediate stages, because that's where I get disheartened. I've noticed that clients in therapy often want to throw in the towel at this midpoint. When that happens, I use this image. It's like being in a small boat that you push off from shore, rowing into the engulfing sea. All you see before you are swells of water. The farther you row, the less land you see behind you, until you are surrounded only by ocean on all sides. You row and row, but still no sight of land before you. You become impatient and discouraged and even start to doubt that dry land is ahead. You slow down and the waves push you backward. You just want to give up.

Although it's natural to grow impatient on the way to something new or unknown, we have to remember that not seeing dry land is part of the process of getting to it. When you're feeling lost and hopeless, knowing that progress is composed of the stages of inability, uncertainty, and floundering can boost your confidence to plow ahead.

Midway is where most of us give up on our goals because all we can see is how far we have to go. At this point things seem to slow down, and we start to have setbacks. Three tips will carry you through to your goal. First, look at how far you have come instead of how far you have to go. This will give you a truer picture of the map of your progress. In other words, acknowledge the five pounds you've lost instead of focusing on the stubborn ten that hang on. If you're working on reducing your angry outbursts, note the progress you've made in reducing it, not the fact that it still happens. Make your barometer the progress you've made, not the perfection of reaching the goal. If you're trying to improve a relationship, ask, "Are things better?" not "Are things perfect?" If things are better, then you're moving forward.

Second, know beforehand that at the midpoint of your progress you might start to feel stuck. That's because progress is a gradual process that occurs in unseen degrees. The small steps we make slowly mount up over time, just as brooks make rivers and rivers run into seas. Your weight might start to level off, and you could go a week without losing pounds. Your relationship might start to feel as if it's going nowhere, making you feel discouraged.

Third, midway is where setbacks start to occur naturally. I guarantee that you will have setbacks if you're trying to reach a goal. What you want to remember here is that falling backward is a natural part of forward progression. Progress is not an unbroken, ascending line. The midpoint is where you might gain an extra pound or two before moving forward again. Or you might lash out at someone, just when you thought you'd overcome the anger outbursts. And your relationships seem to be back at square one again. If, for example, I were to plot the progress in losing weight, improving marital communication, saving money, or exercising, the line would zigzag upward and backward, gradually forming an upward spiral. Sometimes we have to take three steps back before leaping ten steps ahead.

Remember that in your eagerness to arrive at a destination, you cannot skim over the middle stages as if they don't count. On days when you feel you've relapsed or lost sight of your goal, the best strategy I know is to look back and acknowledge how far you've come. The other thing to do is to reframe the setback as an opportunity to strengthen whatever it is that you're working on: your willpower, your relationship, or your emotional control. The more patient you are and the more you let things progress gradually, the more you'll notice how much you can enjoy the journey on the way to your destination. And you'll immediately feel more relaxed as you start to accept and appreciate that the lows are steps that are just as essential and natural to progress as the highs.

Make Up Your Mind to Be Happy

Most folks are about as happy as they make up their minds to be.

—Abraham Lincoln

Many of us want to be someplace we're not. When we're at home, we want to be at the beach. At the beach, we long to be back in our own beds again. The Israeli leader Golda Meir once said, "At work, you think of the children you have left at home. At home, you think of the work you've left unfinished. Such a struggle is unleashed within yourself. Your heart is rent." We seek distant lands in search of happiness, and when we don't find it there, we look elsewhere. Unfortunately, moving across country won't help us find ourselves. We carry our old habits like luggage wherever we go. If we wake up feeling positive and optimistic in Detroit, we wake up feeling positive and optimistic in the Mediterranean. If we wake up anxious and pessimistic in Buffalo, we wake up anxious and pessimistic in the South Pacific.

Everyone wants to live a happy life. So why are so many of us miserable so much of the time, constantly searching for serenity and calm with little success? Because we're looking in the wrong place. In our pursuit of happiness, one thing is for sure. In an effort to fill the void, worldly achievements, material comforts, and financial rewards elbow their way into our minds and become barriers that keep happiness at arm's length.

Scientists and spiritual leaders agree on few things, but one thing they do agree on is that money can't buy happiness. The studies on happiness show that things like wealth, weather, marital status, age, and beauty do not make people any happier—even though most people think they would. Physically attractive people are not happier and people with disabilities aren't more miserable. Happiness is not a by-product of life circumstances, but a by-product of our state of mind—the ways in which we think about our lot in life.

A case in point. Clay said to me, "I want a wife, three kids, a picket fence, and a normal life. That's all it would take for me to be happy." That's what he thought and that's what kept him from being happy: trying to make life fit his image of what it had to be in order for him to be happy, instead of him fitting into what life had in store. This approach is like trying to fit a size nine foot into a size seven shoe. Clay had already proved his way wouldn't work, because he'd already been married three times and had just ended an abusive relationship with a fourth woman. Happiness cannot be dependent on the actions of another person, a series of events, or a particular outcome. Instead of following a mental picture of what we think happiness is, we have to reverse the formula. First we make our mind up to be happy no matter what, and then happiness will take its own natural form, perhaps even greater than what we'd imagined.

A basic Buddhist teaching is that you already have everything you need to be happy, like the old woman who, looking for her eye glasses, realized they were on her nose the whole time. Happiness is a state of mind that has to be cultivated. You can think of a happy state of mind as a muscle, because the more you use it, the stronger it gets. The more you wait around for an event or person to bring it to you, the weaker it gets and the more dependent your happiness is on what happens in the random daily events of your life.

Some of us get so caught up in what we do in the outer world, we don't know who we are on the inside. Is your life stuck in fast-forward and focused on the outside world? Does your constant activity keep you disconnected from yourself, preventing you from knowing who you are? If unhappiness and discontent are created on the inside, doesn't it make sense that to change your life you must start there? Once you look within yourself, you discover what you've been looking for all along. The answers will come to you when you put yourself under the proper conditions: meditation, prayer, contemplation, and mental relaxation. These practices can help you achieve the answers you seek.

You can look at your life in a different way and see things with new insights and greater clarity. You may keep the same job and the same relationship. You may still get angry and impatient, and there will be occasions when you will feel sad or disappointed. But you won't stumble around searching for the answers like the old lady looking for her glasses. Instead, you see what is already yours right in front of your eyes.

Stick Your Neck Out

Success consists of getting up just one more time than you fall.

—Oliver Goldsmith

A friend of mine says she doesn't like to do anything at which she cannot be successful. She says it gives her a feeling of satisfaction to do things perfectly. At work she avoids certain responsibilities and challenges for fear of not doing them well. She won't go white-water rafting or swimming because she'd feel foolish learning how. Here's what she told me in her own words:

"I've only done the things that I felt I could just step in and do well right away. I can't swim because as an adult it's embarrassing to go and learn how to swim. That just kills me. The only way I could do it is if they would clear the pool so nobody could witness my being inept as an adult in something that almost everybody else knows how to do."

Were you the kind of child who had to swim the first time you hit water? Are you the type of adult who only accepts challenges in which you can shine right from the start? Do you avoid those challenges that require that you learn from your own mistakes? If so, your attempts to avoid failure will turn into the avoidance of success. Unfortunately, that's what happened to my friend. She feels she hasn't achieved what she'd hoped in her personal and professional life. The reason is that she hasn't taken the necessary risks for success.

Faced with fear of failure, how many of us walk away? I certainly have. Of course when we walk the other way we put limits on our potential to be successful, and fear wins the battle. The key to winning this battle with fear is to realize that success is automatically guaranteed. The simple act of stepping up and facing the fear of failure, regardless of the outcome of your attempts, means that you have achieved success. With this attitude you cannot possibly lose, because you have conquered self-doubt.

Have you ever had an experience where you've felt the fear and done it anyway? Remember the feelings of calm that descend over you after it's all over? You always win, because you were courageous enough to stick your neck out. As Amelia Earhart put it, "Courage is the price life extracts for granting peace." Public speaking has been as challenging for me as crossing the Atlantic was for Earhart. I remember, after winning an undergraduate award for my field research, my anthropology professor asking me to present the folktales I had collected to her graduate class. Fear elbowed its way into my mind all week. The night of my talk, I went to the classroom a few hours early and set up my tape recorder. Then I sat and stared at the bare walls, drummed my fingers on desktops, and checked my watch a hundred times a minute. I was scared to death that I would be a dismal failure, even though I had already won an award for my work. Realizing that I still had an hour's wait until class time, the suspense got the best of me, and I succumbed to the fear. Feeling defeated, I packed up my equipment and left, later telling the professor that I had gotten sick. I had failed. I was miserable.

Thirty years later, as a professor, author, and psychotherapist, much of what I do is speaking before groups. The way I got here was by feeling the fear and doing it anyway. Most of the time when I speak, fear accompanies me. But I make it sit at my feet now instead of letting it hover over me. And each time I finish a speaking engagement, I feel successful, not because my performance is all that great, but because I beat the fear. I won. Winning in this way brings me true success and genuine peace of mind.

The road to success is paved with a series of fears and failures. Once you can start to accept them as natural and essential stepping-stones to success, you can give yourself permission to make the mistakes necessary to get where you want to go. You can start by identifying a fear that has crippled you or prevented you from succeeding. It can be as small as learning to swim or balancing your checkbook or as big as speaking your mind before a group of peers, confronting someone over a wrongdoing, or launching into a new business venture of your own. Find just one place in your life where you can stick your neck out. As you face and move through your fear, you will feel filled with your inner strength, develop greater confidence in yourself, and stretch one lap closer to the success you have been avoiding.

Diminish Your Wants Instead of Increasing Your Needs

My crown is in my heart, not on my head; not deck'd with diamonds and Indian Stones, nor to be seen: my crown is called content; a crown it is that seldom kings enjoy.

—William Shakespeare

Every time I get together with certain wealthy friends of mine, they're involved in acquiring something new and different. First it was a new swimming pool and for months all their conversations, thoughts, and behaviors were centered around the planning and building of the pool. Since it was built, it has rarely been mentioned and hardly ever used. Instead they moved on to focus on a completely new project of building a mountain home. Blueprints, fabric, and landscaping were the talk in the months to come. Next it was two or three expensive cars, a new guest house, and a new beach bungalow. The mountain home was practically never inhabited and was eventually sold so they could buy a place in the Caribbean and travel the world. Both of them told me that they were deeply unhappy with themselves and each other and couldn't figure out why. They hoped to find contentment in the material things they could afford and the exotic places they could go. But they never did. As far as I know, they are still traveling the world and searching.

When we think of happiness only in terms of what we want, we are operating from a position of lack and discontent. We are focusing on what is missing from our lives and the mind is fooled into thinking that more of *something* or *someone* will fill that void and make us complete. Of course, it doesn't work that way. First of all, whatever we focus on expands, so wanting only increases the feeling that our lives are lacking. And we want more and more to satisfy the hunger. Want and desire are bottomless pits. They will always be there on the sidelines of our lives—pushing us to overspend, overeat, and overindulge ourselves. And indulging our wants and desires still doesn't fulfill us, because a day or week later there's something else that we *must* have.

The cure for this insatiable hunger is contentment. The Dalai Lama says in his book, *The Art of Happiness* (Dalai Lama and Cutler 1998), "The true antidote of greed is contentment. If you have a strong sense of contentment, it doesn't matter whether you obtain the object or not; either way, you are still content." He says there are two ways to reach contentment. One is to acquire everything we want and desire: an expensive house, sporty car, perfect mate, gourmet foods, fashionable clothes, exotic trips, perfectly toned body. The problem with this approach is that sooner or later there will be something that we want but can't have. The second and more reliable approach to contentment is to want and feel grateful for what we already have.

You really do already have everything you need to be happy. Happiness is yours when you start to *want* what you already have instead of *have* what you want. How many times a day do you stop and give thanks for the blessings you do have? Your loved ones who have their health, the food on your table, the shelter over your head, and the special people who touch your life. You can see, hear, think, walk, and enjoy this beautiful day that lies before you! You're alive! And that's more than many people can say. Counting your blessings and being grateful for all that you already have can turn your outlook around. An attitude of gratitude turns pessimism into optimism, helps you see the glass as half full instead of half empty, and helps you see the good in everything that comes your way.

The way to achieve wanting what you have is by naming all the things around you that you're grateful for. Try the gratitude exercise for one entire day: as your feet touch the floor in the morning, on the drive to and from work, as you look into the face of the loved ones who cause your heart to leap with joy, and before drifting off to sleep at night. Be conscious of all the wonderful blessings that you forgot you had or took for granted. Instead of complaining about what you need, express gratitude for all the riches that you already have, and notice the difference it makes in your life. When you want what you already have and express gratitude for it, your life becomes full, satisfying, and complete. And your life is transformed so that you start to see and experience the happiness and abundance that is all around you.

5

Treat Yourself With Love and Respect

I find that when we really love and accept and approve of ourselves exactly as we are, then everything in life works.

—Louise Hay

Always Be There for Yourself

The necessity of appearing in your face. There are days when that is the last place in the world where you want to be but you have to be there, like a movie, because it features you.

—Richard Brautigan

Growing up, I always had a terrible fear of the dentist. Back in the fifties, painless technology didn't exist. To make matters worse, my dentist looked like Bela Lugosi and he was mean! Being in his chair was like being a victim in a grade-B horror flick. When children cried in fear, he actually yelled and sometimes even slapped kids to calm them down. So you can imagine my terror of this drill-wielding, Dracula look-alike heading toward my mouth, mumbling, "Open wide."

But there was one consolation for my fear. My father always stood by my side, offering his big hand for my small, sweaty palm to squeeze as hard as I wanted. Somehow knowing he was there for me always eased the fear and pain a little.

These memories rushed through my mind the day my father lay near death and the nurse called the family in to be with him. This time I held his hand in mine. He was too weak to squeeze it, so I did the squeezing for both of us. All I could do was tell him I loved him, and that everything would be okay. We had traded places—I had become the comforter. When the flatline appeared on the monitor, I could only hope that my words and my hand wrapped tightly around his limp, sweaty palm were as comforting to him as his had been to me.

Today these memories return every time I visit my dentist. My fear of dentists has subsided for the most part, but when it does rear its ugly head, I'm able to be a strong father for that scared little boy inside. I try to be available for myself as my father had so valiantly been for me and as I had tried to be for him. But one time I forgot this lesson when I really needed it the most. I had abandoned myself and didn't even realize it at first.

I told you earlier about my apprehension about public speaking. Well, my greatest life lesson and opportunity to face the fear and do it anyway came with an invitation to appear on *Good Morning America*. After the producer interviewed me and invited me to come, I put the phone down and felt a jolt of panic. "What have you done?" I scolded myself. "Have you lost your mind? What makes you any more knowledgeable about this topic than millions of other people?" Fear began to erode my confidence. I felt as though my mind had catapulted me into a cesspool of dread, and my next few days were spent floundering around in it. Then a realization hit me like a ton of bricks: I had left that scared little boy alone on the front lines, shuddering in his boots. What would my father do if he were still alive? He'd put his arms around me, tell me how proud he was, and give me a pep talk. Once I realized what I'd done, I embraced that little boy, shielded him from fear, and took charge of the situation. I reminded myself that, like my father, I too am a grown, intelligent, well-educated, and capable man. The strength I felt from this inner support overcame my tension. The show came off without a hitch. But the best news of all was that the gift my father had given me continued to live on inside of me.

This type of self-love and self-care has been essential in getting me through lots of tough times—particularly when I neglect myself and begin to suffer the consequences of doing too much. Self-care makes it possible for us to give more care and love to others. You, too, can nurture yourself within your heart in this way. You can comfort that small child inside and reassure him or her that you will always be there. You can be emotionally available for yourself the way your parents were once emotionally present for you. Or you can nurture yourself even if your parents never did.

One helpful strategy is to think about what you would have liked your parents to say and do, then say and do those things for yourself when you face daily challenges. Perhaps your parents were loving and gentle and there's nothing you'd change about them. If so, think of an incident, such as my dentist example, when one or both parents supported you unconditionally. Use this image during tough times and switch places with your parent—treating yourself with that same loving kindness that you got when you were young. Always remember that you have the power within you to endure any situation, because you have yourself—and that's plenty to get you through.

Stand Up to Your Inner Critic

I wouldn't want to belong to a club that would want to have me as a member.

—Groucho Marx

One day as I walked down the hallway of the university where I teach, I saw Karen, my colleague and friend and greeted her with "Namaste" (pronounced NAH-MA-STAY) which is an Indian greeting that loosely means, "hello." Never having heard that word and misunderstanding its meaning, she looked at me with horror in her eyes and said, "My mistake? What did I do wrong?"

This chance encounter led to a lengthy story of Karen's inner critic, a lifelong and haunting companion, born from her parents' motto for the family: "Your best is always better yet." They believed that no matter how hard you work or how well you do, you could work harder, earn more, do better. They would complain that an A- on her report card should have been an A+. When she won a writing contest her father even said to her, "They must not have had too many entries to pick yours." Karen shuttered at the memory of traveling home after her high school graduation—not just because there had been a late spring snow and it was cold outside but because of her mother's chilly reception. Despite the fact that Karen had been honored for having the second highest grade-point average among two thousand students, her mother had been distant and unenthusiastic all day long. As the tires crushed the icy road beneath them, Karen's mother finally broke the ice inside the car: "Why couldn't you have been number one?" she demanded.

In childhood we develop our thoughts and feelings about ourselves from messages we receive from grown-ups. These messages—good and bad, accurate and inaccurate—form our sense of self-confidence or self-doubt. Once grown, the messages continue to play in our minds like tape recordings. Unfortunately, the mental chitchat that causes us to doubt ourselves often gets more play than the tape that tells us how great we really are!

Now that she is grown, Karen's critical parents live on inside her head. Their voices comprise an inner critic who puts her under a microscope, just like her parents did. This critic's job is to disguise her successes as failures and judge her harshly and unmercifully for the most minute flaws. Karen has a deep-seated need to prove herself, and if she makes a mistake or doesn't do something well enough in her own view, she comes down hard on herself. Anytime she takes care of herself, she feels guilty and undeserving. Her inner critic says, "Taking all that time for yourself? You should be at home baking bread, doing house-work, or being with your kids." The price she pays for this self-critique is feeling like a fail-ure most of the time because she has established unreachably high standards for herself. Anytime she sets a goal and actually achieves it, she thinks, "That wasn't worth it; that was nothing." So she creates a higher goal, which she cannot possibly attain.

Good self-esteem is a state of mind. Henry Ford once said, "If you think you can or you can't, you're right." The starting point is to change how you think about yourself. When you let go of the old, inaccurate messages about yourself that you still carry from the past and replace them with supportive affirmations, you'll start to think of yourself as a winner instead of a loser. You'll start to see yourself honestly by recognizing your accom-plishments along with your defeats, your strengths as well as your faults. You'll start to see the inner critic as a mere tape of the past, a mere thought with no real power.

The next time you catch yourself listening to that discouraging voice that blinks in your mind like a neon sign, stand up to it and its impossible standards and judgments. Instead of attacking yourself, think of yourself as a close friend. Replace the inner critic with a friendly voice that nurtures and encourages you, giving you the kind of heartening pep talks you would give to a dear friend. Instead of masking your success with failure, recog-nize and acknowledge your accomplishments for what they are. Take a clear look at your-self and shower yourself with positive affirmations that can help you see the truth about you. The more you look for the positives in yourself, the better you will feel. The more you imagine the best of tomorrow, the better your tomorrow will be.

Don't Judge Your Insides By Someone Else's Outsides

If you want to be respected, the great thing is to respect yourself.

—Fyodor Dostoyevsky

I squeezed myself into the tiny sports car of a psychologist friend who whisked me onto the beltway around St. Louis. We were on our way to meet three other team members with whom we traveled the country speaking at conferences. Our conversation was interspersed with chuckles about a lecture we had given at a St. Louis hospital earlier that day. At the end of the day we all made a mad dash to scope out the audience's evaluations of our presentation. The five of us gathered around a long table and sifted through a pile of one thousand comments. When I pulled out one particularly negative one, the entire group walked away from the stack of positive evaluations, making a circle around me. They listened intently to every word the disgruntled respondent had to say while a stack of 999 glowing comments fell on deaf ears. How much approval is enough? How can one person's criticism outweigh the approval of 999 others? It's easy when you're one in a bunch of perfectionists.

This type of perfectionism has a special name: *telescopic thinking*. The mind acts like a telescope, zooming in and magnifying imperfections while blocking all positive aspects from view. Some of us set our standards so high that no one can meet them—not us, nor our loved ones, friends, or coworkers. Nothing is good enough. Telescopic thinking makes you feel like a perpetual failure even when you're successful, because you constantly put yourself in no-win situations.

You set yourself up to fail when you compare yourself to the tops in each field: the assertiveness of Judge Judy, the creativity of Leonardo da Vinci, the compassion of Mother Teresa, the wit of Rosie O'Donnell, the wealth of Donald Trump, the sex appeal of Mel

Gibson, or the athletic ability of Michael Jordan. When you compare yourself to the best of everything, you'll probably always come up short. Telescopic thinking gives you the illusion that others have what you don't and makes you feel cheated. Even when you excel in three or four areas, you ignore your areas of accomplishment and focus on the ones in which you fall short. Although perceived as outstanding by others, you berate yourself and think of yourself as a failure.

When you use someone else's life as a yardstick to evaluate your own, you judge yourself unfairly. This distorted way of looking at your life prevents you from seeing yourself honestly. The solution is to catch yourself telescoping early, before you go too far. Then put on your wide-angle lens and look at the whole picture of your life—especially the blind spots that your zoom lens shuts out.

A good way to use the wide-angle lens is to identify a worry or criticism you have about yourself first. Perhaps you feel you don't do your best at work, or you worry about being too shy. Now put on your wide-angle lens. Think about the bigger picture and how important your judgment about yourself really is. Think about fifty years from now and what difference this one perceived fault will really make. Probably none. Ask yourself if anyone will die or go to jail as a result of your concerns. Think about a Higher Power or the bigger forces in life: volcanoes, lightning, rain, windstorms, or the vast night sky and consider how important the concern is in the scheme of things. Now as you broaden your outlook on life, how important is the judgment you've made against yourself? If you're like most people, it loses its sting when you put it in a wider perspective.

Seeing yourself truthfully includes acknowledging and affirming your strong qualities, too. Sit down and think of as many positive things about yourself as you can. Consider all the things for which you're grateful and that make your life worth living. Affirm the things that you ordinarily take for granted, the things that if you didn't have them would leave your life empty. Rejoice in your gifts and your uniqueness. Start to see yourself totally, with both your imperfections and your strengths, and begin to think of your limitations as part of your human condition—as aspects of your strength of character rather than personality flaws.

Stop "Shoulding" on Yourself

Words have power; to be specific, your words have power. We can use speech patterns to help us communicate with others in a more considered, conscious way, or we can be careless and create trouble with our words—trouble for ourselves as well as others.

—Lama Surya Das

On more than one cold, rainy night I have caught myself driving to teach a night class thinking, "Why do I have to do this? I'd much rather be a couch potato by the fire right now." Before I know it, I'm feeling resentful that I'm *having* to do something I don't want to do. Then the dread gets even bigger, and I feel consumed by it. I start to resent the job and sometimes even the students.

In these kinds of situations I have learned to pay close attention to my mind's oppressive self-talk—the "have-to's" or "musts." Then I realize it sounds like an outside person or situation is standing over me, making me do something I don't want to do. And that's simply not the case at all. When I get into these negative moods, I rethink the situation. In these particular situations, I remind myself that teaching a night class was my idea. Not only did I agree to teach the class, but I even chose the day and time. The more I realize that nobody was *making* me do anything, the more the resentment and negative attitude start to melt away. I feel that I'm doing something that I wanted to, not that I *had* to, do. I begin to feel empowered instead of victimized by the situation, and my new attitude pulls me out of the negative mood.

The self-talk our minds use to weigh situations shapes our attitudes about them. Words like "should," "ought," "must," and "have to" are words most people use from time to time. And they have a strong effect on our outlook. These words are your personal signature for how you feel inside, and they reveal thought patterns that give power to your feelings and actions. They can cause you to feel guilt, shame, or hopelessness and to feel that you are a slave to your emotions instead of master of them. By asking yourself if your words empower or oppress, you can become more aware of what you say to yourself and choose your words more carefully. You can provide self-support by sending yourself uplifting and comforting words rather than defeating messages.

Use of the word "should," for example, is a method of scolding ourselves: "I should have gone to church on Sunday," or "I should have done better in that tennis game." You can change your self-defeating attitudes by paying attention to the words you use during self-talk. Try this exercise. Name three things you *should* have done in the last week. Finish the incomplete sentence, "I should have _____ ," for each of the three things you named. Now substitute the word "could" for each of your "shoulds" and notice how it changes the meaning of your statement and thus the tone of the message you send to yourself. "Shoulds" are shamed-based messages that generate negative feelings, whereas "coulds" indicate that you made a choice and you simply *chose* to do one thing and not the other.

Replacing negative words (such as "must," "have to," "should," "ought") with empowering words (such as "could," "want to," "can," "choose to") can change your feelings of being at the mercy of a situation to being in charge of it. Feeling in charge, in turn, helps you feel more positive about things. And the truth is that we choose most things anyway—even when it feels like we have no choice in the matter.

Start to think of yourself as your best friend and treat yourself that way. When you're feeling defeated, use uplifting words that encourage you. When you're riddled with self-doubt, give yourself pep talks. When you're scared, use comforting language.

Your words have power, so make it a point to use them in a positive, supportive way. Start to ask yourself if your language supports your inner self or condemns and oppresses it. And as you begin to treat yourself with the same love, kindness, and consideration that you give to others you care about, you'll notice that it boosts your self-confidence and your well-being.

Affirm Yourself

D O I O O I O O I O O I O

*At bottom every man knows well enough that he is a unique being, only once on this
earth; and by no extraordinary chance will such a marvelously picturesque piece of
diversity in unity as he is, ever be put together a second time.*

—Friedrich Wilhelm Nietzsche

Sometimes I can be driving along and see a bicyclist or runner and notice what great shape
they're in and then amplify their accomplishments into defeat for myself. I don't realize I'm
doing it. But instead of saying to myself, "How great for them," I start to examine my flaws
and to compare my fifty-year-old belly to a twenty-year-old washboard stomach. How
unfair that is to me! Of course, when I catch myself, I realize the important thing is to learn
to accept my body, my age, and myself—my unique self.

We get only one body in this go-around called life. No one else will ever look through
these eyes, feel with this heart, or touch with these hands—no one but you. No one will ever
experience life in exactly the same way. You are a marvelous bundle of diversity and unity.
How lucky you are to have this once-in-a-lifetime chance to live your life in this body. There
will never be another person uniquely constructed in exactly the same way as you or me.

Although I think it's important to stay in as good shape as I can, I'm also learning to
accept my love handles and my gray. You can start to accept your emotional and physical
uniqueness by sending yourself balanced, positive messages and by reversing that inner
critical voice that replays your faults like a CD wired into the brain. Positive affirmations
help you recognize and appreciate your true value. Affirming your eye color or bald spots
and expressing gratitude for your physical body just as it is can help you begin to feel better
about yourself.

Here are a few affirmations that you can choose, cafeteria-style, if you like. Pick the
ones that resonate most with you or that bring you calm. Or use these as examples and

write your own, tailoring them to your unique self and situation. Then continue to repeat your affirmations silently to yourself.

* *I am grateful for the unique person that I am. I value all my physical and personal qualities, which are uniquely me. They are _____ (fill in the blanks).*

* *My worth doesn't depend on everyone liking me. Things do not have to be perfect for me to be happy. I accept myself as I am. I am coming to see my true value. I am loving and affirming myself more and more each day.*

* *My happiness comes from within, not from the outside. I do not depend on the outer world to make me happy. I do not need anything or anyone beyond what I already have to make me happy. I have everything I need for happiness to fill my life. Wanting what I have makes me happy and leaves me fulfilled. Today I no longer look for something or someone to make me feel complete. I am at peace with myself.*

* *When I count my blessings, I see that I have much more to be thankful for than to fret about. Life is full of disappointments, but I choose to experience them as lessons that build inner fortitude and a stronger foundation for my personal growth.*

* *My value as a human being begins with me today through my own self-acceptance and self-love.*

There are many ways to use affirmations. You can write them down and repeat them to yourself over and over again. You can record them on tape and play them back, or put them up in strategic places around your house. The bathroom mirror or your personal computer are good places where you'll see the affirmation early and often. One of my favorites for the mirror says: *You are looking at the only person in the world who can determine your happiness.*

I challenge you to affirm, love, and respect yourself. Be yourself. Pamper yourself. Forgive and care for yourself. Enjoy your own company and be your own best friend. Do the things for *you* that you would do for the ones you love the most. As you do, so will you be!

Acknowledge Your Tallcomings
Along with Your Shortcomings

Humility is the truth about ourselves loved.

—G. Carey-Elwes

A friend of mine takes compliments and turns them into insults against herself. When someone told her how nice her new haircut looked, she said, "Are you kidding? Are you making fun of me? It looks like a mop!" When friends complimented her on her work, she snapped, "Stop making fun of what I did. I know it's not as good as yours, but I'm doing the best I can." This woman was dishonest because she saw *only* the worst in herself and could not affirm her good. She either treated herself as if she were inferior to others or she acted superior to them. Both attitudes stem from a feeling of inequality.

Do you blush when someone praises you? Do you feel discomfort when you're applauded for a kind deed? Do you feel awkward when someone compliments you on how you look? Compliments are sometimes hard to accept, especially when you cannot acknowledge the good in yourself. You may find it easier to accept negative comments and put-downs because they more closely match how you feel about yourself. Many of us, because we are so used to criticism, feel more comfort with it than praise. But that's not the whole truth about ourselves.

The importance of humility and modesty is pounded into most of our heads from childhood, and indeed they are character strengths. Somehow as adults, though, we get that message confused with using put-downs about ourselves as a measure of humility. Then we adopt fault finding and self-condemnation as standards for character strength.

It has been said that the first and worst of all frauds is to cheat oneself. Self-deception is the refusal to see things as they truly are, as if we looked through the objective eyes of an outsider. It causes us to deny ourselves the same loving kindness and self-respect that we give to others. We may not be aware that we go about our days collecting evidence of our flaws like catching butterflies in a net. At the end of the day we sort and classify our collection. We assemble and reassemble negative comments, defeats, and mistakes as we would arrange dried insects on a board. We examine our collection of evidence inside out, upside down, and right side up. We replay every negative comment and every bad feeling. But what about the ones that got away? Had we aimed our net in another direction, we would have a collection of compliments, successes and joys to sort and classify too. We could spend the rest of the day examining these specimens from every possible angle as well. But we are not used to collecting items that allow us to love the truth, the whole truth, and nothing but the truth about ourselves.

It is important to acknowledge and take responsibility for mistakes and human imperfections. Knowing and addressing your human limitations and downfalls is a character strength that can be used to your advantage. But for an honest assessment of yourself, it's also important to balance your shortcomings with your "tallcomings." Seeing yourself truthfully includes acknowledging all the good things about yourself. You can overcome self-deception by being more aware of *both* your strong points and areas for improvement, by not putting yourself down, and by treating yourself with the same love and respect that you give to others.

Ask yourself if you're more comfortable living the life of an underdog than you are living on top. Are you so accustomed to struggle and heartache that you're uncomfortable with profit and happiness? Next, be aware of the kinds of evidence about yourself that you collect during a day. Do you focus on the all-too-familiar faults? Or do you hold out for the rare positive evidence that gives you greater value and more honest feedback about who you are? Start taking compliments from others into your heart without false pride or false modesty. Learn to accept compliments as a way of seeing the truth about yourself, instead of ignoring them or letting them sail over your head. As you get to know yourself more truthfully, you get to know all of humanity better. And you will feel more connected, more relaxed, and more content within yourself.

Stand Up for Yourself

People seldom want to walk over you until you lie down.

—Elmer Wheeler

This is the story of Simon, the girlfriend, and the professors. Simon let people walk all over him. His girlfriend called the shots in their relationship, and he let her. Otherwise, he said, he'd catch hell. He split his time as a graduate assistant between three professors for twenty hours a week. Each one expected him to be there for them, so he ended up working forty-hour work weeks but got paid for only twenty. One professor expected Simon to give up weekends to assist him in his research lab. Unable to get his schoolwork done, Simon had to abolish his social life in order to meet the work schedule of the professors.

Simon was resentful toward his girlfriend and the professors. His solution? He fantasizes about telling his girlfriend to drop dead and his professors to stick their research where the sun doesn't shine. But these feelings of anger kept him paralyzed in passivity, and he did nothing. What's wrong with this picture? The professors were not at fault, because Simon hadn't explained his circumstances to them. So they kept asking for his time, and Simon kept giving it. He said he was afraid to say no because it might affect his grades or his status in the department. Simon really was not afraid of getting bad grades; he knows his stuff. He was afraid to stand up to the people in his life.

When he tried to stand up for himself, Simon's choices teetered between catering to people on the one hand and steamrolling them on the other. In my view, neither extreme is acceptable. Still, sucking it up and complying with other people's wishes usually wins out for many of us because it feels safer. The problem is that it keeps us resentful and doesn't take care of our needs. A midpoint somewhere in between these extremes will protect others from your wrath and protect you from your neglect. Here are a few steps to follow when you need to be assertive.

Step one: Take time out. If someone asks you to do something that you feel is unreasonable or inconvenient, don't back yourself in a corner and give an immediate answer. You'll be making a decision under pressure and will probably say yes to something to which you really want to say no. Then you'll be mad at yourself and the person making the request. Instead, tell the person you'll check your schedule and get back with them. That buys you time to think about what *you* want to do and the best way to say it.

Step two: Discuss it with yourself in private. Make a pact that you will stop doing things that are unfair to yourself. Try not to blame others when you feel they make an unreasonable request (it may not seem unreasonable to them) or have not honored a line that you haven't drawn. It's up to each of us to tell others where that line is and when we feel like they've crossed it. Make your decision, and practice informing the other person calmly and matter-of-factly without making apologies or excuses.

Step three: Inform the other party. Use assertiveness—that midpoint on a spectrum with passivity on one end and aggressiveness on the other. Suppose, for example, someone asks you to help them move on your only Saturday off in a month. You tell them that you will check your schedule and get back to them. After you've given it some thought (about three seconds), you decide that you need that day for yourself. You inform the other party in a calm and genuine, but matter-of-fact manner with something like, "Gosh, I would like to help you out, but I've already made other plans for that day." And you probably *would* like to help them out, but not at your expense. And you do have other commitments: *to yourself*.

Standing up for yourself, whether to a friend, loved one, or colleague doesn't have to be frightening or combative. It can be smooth and direct. The interesting part about being assertive is that people respect you for it. Simon noticed that, as he became more assertive with his girlfriend, she responded favorably and actually started treating him better. And he discovered that the professors were more than happy to oblige about his schedule.

There's an old saying that we teach others how to treat us by how they see us treat ourselves. The best way to stand up for yourself is to treat yourself with consideration and respect. I promise you the people around you will follow your lead.

Take a Vacation Instead of a Guilt Trip

Guilt is the prosecutor who knows how to make every victim feel like the criminal.
—Ruth Gendler

A man returned from work one day and was delighted to discover a large package waiting on his porch. The gift was meticulously wrapped in purple and green and he wondered who would be sending him such an elaborate, lovely surprise. He eagerly set about opening it—only to find that the address on the box wasn't his. It belonged to a neighbor a few houses down the street.

Disappointed, he set the package in a corner where it would be safe, telling himself he would deliver it himself later in the day. A few days later, having gotten caught up in his own busy life, the package still set there. As he opened the newspaper, he read that the neighbor to whom the package was addressed had died. Suddenly, he was overwhelmed by waves of crushing guilt. How could he have been so cruel to withhold something from this dying man that could have brought him joy in his last moments? How could he have deprived the ones who mailed the package from sharing their love one last time?

In another situation a woman who is a big giver has trouble receiving. Her favorite aunt died and left her a lot of money. This was an aunt whom she dearly loved and cared for both as a child and as a grown-up while her aunt was in a nursing home. But she was overcome with tremendous guilt for taking the inheritance. What she failed to see was that the guilt and reticence to accept her aunt's money was actually a rebuff of her aunt's expression of love.

Some guilt is good, because it reminds us to do the right thing. But when carried too far, it can be one of the most powerful, though common, poisons of the mind. Guilt is a verdict that we render against ourselves for the smallest offense. No matter how "good" we try to be, if we look hard enough, we can always find some reason to embark on a guilt-trip. But what we are actually doing is punishing ourselves because, deep down, we believe that we're essentially undeserving.

Both people in the examples blamed themselves for things that were circumstantial and beyond their control. It's admirable to take responsibility for our part. But guilt is not valid when we blame ourselves for things that are truly not our fault. The man who received the package was not the one who mislabeled it, he was not the one who misdelivered it, and he was not the one who caused the man to die at this coincidental time. The woman who'd inherited had nothing to feel guilty about because she had done nothing but give to her aunt her whole life. Accepting the money was a way of respecting her aunt's wishes. True love is not based just on giving. We have to be willing to receive as well, or the circle is incomplete.

Have you been guilt-tripping yourself about something for which you are truly not responsible? I used to have a lot of trouble with this, so I finally made a pact with myself that I will not imprison myself unfairly with guilt or shame. One of the things I do when I feel guilty about something is ask myself if I caused it, can control it, or can cure it. If the answer is yes to any of the three, I take responsibility to correct and make amends for the problem. But more often than not the answer is no. In that case I feel the sadness and compassion for those involved and let go of the guilt, because this kind of guilt is self-destructive and unproductive.

If you have been blaming yourself unfairly for something that you did not cause, cannot control, or cannot cure, acquit yourself with a verdict of "not guilty." You can feel and express remorse for the ones involved and still release yourself from the prison of guilt. If you try this exercise, you will notice a big difference in how you feel. You are actually expressing an act of honesty, fairness, and honor to yourself and to those involved. So the next time you start to take a guilt trip, give yourself a break and let your mind take a vacation instead!

Throw a Party Instead of a Fit

If you are patient in one moment of anger, you will escape a hundred days of sorrow.

—Chinese Proverb

Hair and fingernails were flying everywhere! Not really. But it felt like it. I was having one of those uncontainable anger fits because somebody had rubbed me the wrong way. You know what I mean. Surely you've had one before. Someone says the wrong thing at the wrong time and you blow!

The building where my private practice is located has a tiny parking lot with assigned parking. One day a new tenant moved in and on the first day helped herself to her parking spots and ours, too. I kindly reminded her about the assigned parking, but she seemed to disregard what I had to say.

The next day it happened again, and our clients started complaining of having no place to park. When our secretary politely reminded the new tenant, the woman snapped at her, saying she was too busy to talk to her. The next day as I was leaving for lunch, the woman, who was being formed in my mind as "the nasty tenant," parked her car in one of my spaces and got into someone else's car. I stopped her and gently reminded her that she was parked in my space. She started ranting and raving, screaming how unreasonable I was and that there was plenty of parking. Then she lit into me, yelling across the parking lot what a horrible person I was and how I had no business practicing psychotherapy. She didn't know it, but she had hit my hot button—my credibility. It takes a lot to get me riled up, but this time I came back with all guns blazing! I don't remember what I yelled back, but I do remember the fearful look on her face when I threatened to have her car towed and a few other things I'm too embarrassed to admit. Let's just say she quickly jumped into her car and moved into one of her spaces, and we never had that problem again.

The worst part of this anger fit was that I was left with an emotional hangover that felt horrible. It's that feeling you get after you've had too much to drink, and you can't take it back. I was not proud that I'd lost control or of what I had said. We sounded like two children having a schoolyard disagreement. I was angry at myself for not handling the situation in a more rational and professional manner. On the other hand, I reminded myself that, as a member of the human race, I'm entitled to my share of mistakes.

Anger is a natural human emotion. It's as valid as joy or sorrow. When things don't go our way, it naturally hurts, disappoints, and frustrates us. We may scream, curse, or sulk. We may even rant and rave, stomp our feet, and throw things like children who don't get their way. When anger grips your soul, the important thing is to express it in a healthy way. If you keep angry feelings to yourself, you only recycle the same thoughts through your mind and the feelings get stronger inside you.

If you find yourself angry a lot you can ask, "What incident or person has hurt me?" You can identify the pain and feel the feelings—and begin to heal. The masquerading anger will disappear as you experience your hurt and let the feelings flow in a safe and private place. Expressions of anger through constructive outlets—such as talking with a trusted friend or counselor, writing down feelings in a diary, or pounding an old tennis racket on a mattress—can help release negative feelings so that you can express them constructively through words. One of the best ways to do this is to write a catharsis letter. *Catharsis* means release. The purpose of a catharsis letter is to get out your anger and to give it the energy it deserves instead of keeping it bottled up. But this is not a letter to send to the person toward whom you're angry. It is a letter for your eyes and your eyes only. Start with "Dear ____" (name the person or situation). Then start writing nonstop as fast as you can without taking your pen off the paper. Don't censor your feelings or edit your thoughts. Don't try to make sense of what you put down. Remember this letter is only for your eyes and no one else's. Once you're through, put the letter in a private place or better yet, destroy it. It has already served its purpose.

You can repeat this exercise again and again, addressing the same person or situation, until you feel you've gotten all your feelings out. Once you get your anger on paper, you'll be surprised at how much better you feel. You'll feel more like throwing a party instead of a fit.

Replace "What If's" with "What Is"

Never bear more than one kind of trouble at a time. Some people bear three kinds: all they have had, all they have now, and all they expect to have.

—Edward Everett Hale

Flames engulfed our tiny wood-frame house. It was 1950, and I was five years old. I remember standing, paralyzed by fear, as the fire roared and swelled. My older sister and I huddled together in terror as neighbors worked frantically to retrieve household goods. Minutes before, I had witnessed flames leaping up the kitchen wall and my mother's sharp demands for me to hurry out as she desperately tried to douse them. And I vaguely remember my mother's moans of horror after head-counting her three children and realizing that her eighteen-month-old daughter was still inside the burning house. Later we discovered that my older sister had picked up the baby sister and carried her to safety before the fire started burning out of control. But the fire continued to rage until our house burned to the ground. We were left with nothing, except a few pieces of furniture and the clothes on our backs. But that incident also took something else from me—my sense of "what is," replacing it with only "what if?".

Fast forward to 1985. I had purchased an old Victorian house that I would spend the next fifteen years renovating. Every time I left the house, I feared that it would burn down. I would imagine the house ablaze and that when I pulled into the driveway, it would be in smoldering ruins. That old house had survived for a hundred years, so there was no good reason to believe it would suddenly burn to the ground just because I had moved into it. It was purely superstitious thinking, based on "what if's"—the seeds of which were planted in 1950.

Do you continue to be afraid for reasons long past? Does your body still carry the reflex of these old fears—a flip-flop in the stomach, a tightness in the shoulders, a "what if" in the brain? "What if it rains tomorrow?" "What if I don't get this job?" "What if they don't like me?" I don't have to tell you how these intrusive thoughts can interrupt your enjoyment of the present and keep you stuck in the future—a bleak future at that—causing you to miss the present altogether.

Asking ourselves "what if" questions is just another way to generate needless anxiety and crisis in our lives. It's another form of negative thinking that recycles past fears through the present. "It happened once, so what's to stop it from happening again?" Sometimes we worry about things that never even remotely happened to us. We have just developed the *habit* of anxiety. And sometimes we have more comfort with it than we do with peace of mind. If a loved one is late and it's raining, do you imagine the worst thing that could possibly happen and play it out over and over again in your mind? This line of thinking is a way of magnifying concerns so that they grow larger than they really are, like a bad piece of meat that seems to swell the longer you chew it. When you turn "what if's" over and over in your mind, they expand, and your thoughts about them become distorted to the point that you're dealing with a magnification of the problem—not the real problem.

"What if's" are the children of fear. They are manufactured in our minds and almost never come true. They are a way of trying to control an unknown and unpredictable future. The solution is to stop wrapping your emotions around "what if's" and deal with the irrational fear. Think of your "what if's" as a caution light from your mind that something's wrong, like a fever or hiccups signal that something is out of kilter with your body. Instead of ignoring a fever or hiccups, you'd drink water or take proper medication. So instead of allowing "what if's" to run amuck in your mind, go ahead and acknowledge the caution light and take proper precautions. Then dismiss the fear.

A powerful strategy to reduce intrusive "what if's" is to compartmentalize them. In your mind's eye, see yourself putting each one in a box. Imagine placing the lid on the box and putting it on a storage shelf in a basement or attic. Leave the "what if's" there. Take them off the shelf and out of the box only when you plan to give them your full attention and work on them directly. If one of them gets loose, one trick that works is to put a thick rubber band around your wrist. Every time you think "what if," snap the band and say "Stop!" in your mind. Or if you're alone, yell "Stop!" loudly as you snap the rubber band.

When your "what if's" start doing a number on you, enlist the help of "what is" and put the "what if's" out of your mind. Then you'll be ready to face life as it comes, not as you fear it might come.

6

Lead a Balanced Life

There can't be a crisis next week. My schedule is already full.
—Henry Kissinger

Know Where to Draw the Line

*How many things, which for our own sake we should never do,
do we perform for the sake of our friends*

—Marcus Cicero

I heard the sounds of whimpers that grew into a crescendo of moans and wails coming from behind the closed bathroom door.

"Are you okay?" I asked my houseguest.

"Yes," she sniffled. "I'll be out in a minute."

I was too exhausted to express my true concern, having chaired a two-day conference that had just ended the day before. I had gotten up at 5:00 A.M. for the last two mornings, shuffled speakers from hotels to their speaking engagements, listened to strings of complaints from conferees, hosted a dinner party for eight people at my house, and acted as all-around troubleshooter for last-minute glitches.

It was now Saturday morning. The conference had ended, but the real challenge was just beginning. My houseguest was a conference speaker and close friend of mine who, along with her husband and five-year-old son, stayed at my house instead of a hotel.

The wailing continued. My friend had just realized she wasn't pregnant. She emerged from the bathroom in tears and collapsed in my arms. My soothing comments were interrupted by a telephone call from another friend. I reached for the portable phone with one hand, my other arm around my distraught houseguest.

"How's it going?" I asked the caller.

"I'm really bummed out, man," he replied sullenly and proceeded to tell me how he had just broken up with the woman he had planned to marry in two months.

With one friend crying in one ear and the second lamenting in my other, my Lhasa Apso, not to be outdone, stood on hind legs, begging to go outside to pee. Paralyzed, I thought, "How'd I get into this mess?" and "Whom will I have to hurt or disappoint to get out of it?" The answer was, of course, myself. I loved and cared for my friends but was struck with an overwhelming need to have someone put their arms around *me* at that moment. I became soberly aware that I had spent the entire week putting everybody else's needs before my own and how unfair that was to me.

You too may find yourself putting your needs at the bottom of the list from time to time in order to rescue other people from life. You even may be attracted to friends, loved ones, and business associates for whom you feel sorry and who need to be helped. Rescuing keeps the focus off of you and on someone else. You may hear a lecture and think, "Now this is what my spouse or friend needs to hear," instead of absorbing the advice for yourself. If you spend so much time saving others, you probably neglect yourself and end up stunting your own opportunities for growth.

Self-sacrifice is a virtue, so we are told. And putting ourselves last is supposed to be a character strength. I disagree. The truth is that when we fail to eat right, rest, and exercise, we become overly stressed and burnt out, which limits the amount of energy we can give to our jobs, loved ones, and friends. If we think of ourselves as a bank account from which we're always making withdrawals and no deposits, we realize the result can only be emotional and physical bankruptcy. The key to avoid this is making daily deposits by saying "no" when we're already overloaded, making sure we get the right amount of rest, exercise, and nutrition, and by doing things that interest and replenish us. When we take care of ourselves first, we have more to go around.

A colleague asks you to do something you don't want to do and you say no. You speak up when a friend tries to take advantage of your good nature. You refuse to bail a loved one out of trouble for the umpteenth time. Sometimes the best way to care is to self-care by drawing the line to protect yourself. Self-care prepares you to give more love and nurturance to others. When you put yourself first, there's more of you to go around. The difference between caring for others and making yourself a doormat is knowing where to draw the line; this can be one of the best gifts you can give yourself and the people in your life.

Don't Let Your Overdoing Be Your Undoing

They intoxicate themselves with work so they won't see how they really are.
—Aldous Huxley

For years, right before I would leave on vacation, my friends and family would search my bags and confiscate any work I was trying to smuggle to the beach house we had rented. But they would always miss the tightly folded pieces of paper covered with work notes that I had stuffed into the pockets of my jeans. The thought of going on vacation with no work was terrifying to me. When family and friends would ask me to join them for a stroll on the beach, I would say that I was tired and wanted to take a nap. In the empty house, I would pull out my concealed papers and work until I heard the others returning. Then I'd hide the papers again, stretch out on the bed, and pretend to asleep. As I recount this story to you now, it sounds strange to me. But at that time, it had become a way of coping that seemed perfectly normal.

Many people today have the same problem, living with this well-dressed mental-health problem that is supported by the workplace. On the surface the ability to do two or three things at once or to meet impossible deadlines brings honor. To illustrate the pace of work it expects for its employees, one corporation promotes the motto, "We want you to be able to put tires on this car while it's running eighty miles an hour." But this motto side-tracks people from closeness, breaks down communication, and creates stress and burnout that can lead to chronic health problems. Some people enjoy the adrenaline highs, reminiscent of alcoholic euphoria, that they get from trying to get everything squeezed in. But adrenaline-charged binges are often followed by a downward swing in which euphoria gives way to emotional hangovers characterized by withdrawal, depression, irritability, and anxiety. Like other addictions, there's a point at which overdoers hit bottom. Some become so depressed they cannot get out of bed. They find themselves alone, unable to feel, and cut off from everyone they care about. Marriages crumble and health problems climb.

We have an epidemic of people in this country who do too much. "There aren't enough hours in a day," is our motto. The need to put more hours in a day indicates the need to go overboard. We carry this mind-set into work, managing a house, child rearing, exercise, school, hobbies, and even vacations. We think that the more things we can squeeze into twenty-four hours, the better off we are. But that's rarely the case.

If you want to stop overdoing it, you need to recognize that less is more. If you really want to keep your overdoing from undoing you, you'll simplify your life, appreciate how rich your life already is, and recognize that more hours in the day or more things will not bring more happiness. You'll find that you can relax your standards, be realistic about what's possible, and still do a good job.

So whether you're a workaholic or just do too much, here's my four-step self-care plan to help you work to live instead of live to work:

Work moderation. Abstaining from excessive work is the goal here. Try to set a more steady work schedule with regular hours, avoiding "binge working." When possible confine your work to eight hour days, five days a week.

Outside interests. Establish outside links to new friends and new ideas through such things as hobbies, social contacts, and recreation. Expand your interests and talents beyond your daily work role to develop a richer life.

Renewed relationships. Overlooked relationships are often in disarray or defunct. Identify friendships and intimate relationships that have become stale and renew those close ties. Take time to enjoy long walks and heart-to-heart talks with coworkers, friends or loved ones whom you have neglected.

Keen introspection. Take a deep personal inventory into the roots of your drive to overwork, and ask yourself if there's something you're trying to escape from. Sometimes overdoing it can mask a range of feelings from anger and depression to low self-esteem, fear of intimacy, or an obsessive need to control.

Find That Inner Stillness That Will Carry You Through Rough Times

*Within you there is a stillness and sanctuary to which
you can retreat at anytime and be yourself.*

—Hermann Hesse

As a child I remember camp meetings in the South where fireflies punctuated the dark summer sky and believers fanned away the sweltering heat as they gathered under huge tents to worship. I often peeked through slits in the tents to watch the worshipers raise their arms to the heavens, clap their hands, speak in tongues, run up and down aisles, and sometimes cut cartwheels in ecstasy as they became "slain in the spirit." I was amazed and intrigued by what my boyhood eyes saw. Little did I know that these people were engaging in religious practices that were essential to their mental and physical health.

Many people who have experienced moments of deep spirituality will speak of an indescribably powerful natural "high" that accompanied the experience. These natural highs can occur with prayer, meditation, contemplation, or other internal experiences. For some it's the rush from seeing a beautiful sunset. For others it is a meaningful spiritual connection through prayer. And for others it is a heightened bliss from deep meditation or connection with a Higher Power.

Deep within you is a stillness and sanctuary to which you can retreat from today's hectic world to gain insight and peace. These meaningful internal experiences may be important for your survival. They cause biochemical reactions that have special benefits for your health. Scientific studies tell us this: a view of nature from your hospital window can contribute more to your recovery from surgery than certain drugs; people who go to church live longer and healthier lives than those who do not; people who meditate live longer than those who do not; and the power of positive thinking is alive and well in the fact that optimists tend to live longer than pessimists.

Finding quiet in the noise and chaos of the millennium is essential for balanced living. But a certain amount of solitude is a precondition for finding inner calm and stillness, and being alone is something many of us avoid at all costs. We run from solitude and fill our lives with busy pursuits and possessions to keep loneliness at bay. Some of us are afraid of what we might find lurking inside ourselves. If you change your outlook on solitude, you will discover an inward quietness—not of vacancy but of stability and fulfillment. And you will find a resource within you that can help you navigate through stressful days. In the words of Henry David Thoreau, "I never found the companion that was so companionable as solitude."

During quiet, reflective moments, you can gain clarity and find answers to your daily challenges. You can create this inner place of calm, harmony, and contentment anywhere, anytime—at home, in your office, or in some other special place where you can be alone. This contact can be achieved in many ways—from being a nature lover, student of a spiritual discipline, or a regular at church or synagogue. Or you can immerse yourself in an inspirational book, a hot bath, or a craft. Short walks or meditating for a few minutes can help you unwind and clear your head. By taking a few moments to relax each day, stress will not seem so overwhelming and your life will feel more manageable.

Regardless of how you achieve it, the important point is that deep, inner connections are not only the building blocks to your well-being, but they are the building blocks to your being well. You can always go to this inner sanctuary to become refreshed, relaxed, and recharged.

Meditate Instead of Medicate

When one devotes oneself to meditation, mental burdens, unnecessary worries, and wandering thoughts drop off one by one; life seems to run smoothly and pleasantly.

—Nyogen Senzaki

After hours of working around his lake house, Justin sits at the end of each day, looking over his day's work. Instead of basking in the satisfaction of his accomplishments, he sees more that needs to be done. A fence needs a nail. A weed needs pulling. Bare wood needs paint. Restless and unable to relax, he is up and at 'em again while wishing he could just sit and watch the grass grow. The mind can be like Grand Central Station, with thoughts going and coming—thoughts that keep you running all the time, stuffing your day with so many activities and responsibilities that you don't even have a chance to think. What you may be doing is, in effect, medicating yourself with distraction to keep from facing certain painful thoughts. Some do it with alcohol, television, food, and work. The antidote? Meditation instead of medication. So first let me say that the word "meditation" may sound "woo woo" to you. And if it does, I understand. But you don't have to burn incense, sit cross-legged, and chant incantations to meditate. That's a stereotype that sometimes scares people away from one of the most profitable tools available to combat stress and achieve calm. Meditation quiets the mind and is now being used in mainstream medicine to do what we used to rely on drugs to do. Scientists have found that meditation slows down heart rate and brainwave patterns and boosts the immune system and that people who meditate have less stressful lives, are happier, and live longer.

There are many types of meditation: prayer, inspirational readings, relaxation exercises, quiet reflection, yoga, or guided meditation. The following guided meditation was designed to help you pay closer attention to the needs of your body, mind, and spirit. Get comfortable in a relaxed position and a quiet place where you can put yourself fully into this journey. You may want to tape this meditation, pausing where appropriate, with soft music, and play it back later.

> *Get comfortable, uncross your legs, close your eyes. Now focus on your breathing. Take a few deep breaths. Let it all go. Breathe in through the nose and out through the mouth. Again, in through the nose and out through the mouth.*
>
> *Be aware of the seat beneath you, the clothes on your body, and the sounds around you. Let go of your thoughts about what happened earlier today or might happen tomorrow. Don't try to resist whatever comes up, just be aware of your thoughts and let them pass by. Forget about what you have to do after this meditation. Let this be a time just for you.*
>
> *Take a few more deep breaths, inhaling through the nose and exhaling through the mouth. Feel your body becoming completely relaxed from head to toe. Continue breathing and relaxing until you are in a completely relaxed state.*
>
> *Once you are feeling relaxed, visualize yourself going through your day at a slow pace. Take yourself through your daily routine, all the while slowing yourself down. See yourself eating slower, driving slower, and doing one thing at a time. See the events of the day and imagine the smallest details of each one. Release any images you have of hurrying. Notice how you begin to feel as your routine slows down. How do others around you feel?*
>
> *Pay close attention to your body. What does it need that it hasn't been getting? Pay attention to your mind. What does it need that it doesn't get? Pay attention to your spiritual needs (or feelings). What have they been missing? Then visualize yourself attending to these needs.*
>
> *Conclude your meditation by imagining going to bed that night. How do you feel as you drift off to sleep? Don't be discouraged if you initially feel discomfort or even anxiety. Remember, you're changing habits that you've had for a long time. Giving yourself attention and slowing down take time, practice, and patience.*

Repeat this exercise as often as you feel the need.

Get the "Omni" Out of Your Presence

Many could forgo heavy meals, a full wardrobe, a fine house, et cetera; it is the ego they cannot forgo.

—Mohandas Gandhi

I will never forget that beautiful day. It was springtime in the North Carolina mountains. Mountain laurel and dogwoods punctuated the landscape. The sky was Carolina blue with white puffy clouds darting between the mountains. Birds were singing and butterflies played tag in the warm, gentle sunlight. I was visiting a spiritual retreat center and was surrounded with wonderful people—except for one man wearing a long flowing robe, who seemed overly pious and turned every conversation to himself.

When I couldn't contain my bliss any longer, I exclaimed to the group, "What a beautiful day!" The robed man admonished me with, "That's my name, Beautiful Day. Please find another way of expressing your happiness!" Obviously, this man wanted to possess a universal expression that millions of people use every day. "How selfish," I thought. Here was someone on a spiritual path who had become so self-absorbed that he was missing the whole point. Then I remembered the old saying, "EGO stands for Ease God Out."

This entire book stresses the importance of self-examination and self-awareness, both of which are important in order to find ourselves. But the paradox and pitfall of self-discovery is that spending so much time immersed in our own egos and getting so wrapped up in ourselves can make us self-centered. When everything revolves around us and our needs to the exclusion of others, we can lose our ability for compassion and empathy and forget that there are other points of view. The solution is to balance finding ourselves with getting out of ourselves so that we don't get stuck there. In the words of Henry Miller, "Until we lose ourselves, there is no hope of finding ourselves." While self-awareness and self-evaluation are important, you don't want to become overly focused on yourself to the point of being self-centered.

The key is to be aware of the difference between selflessness, self-care, and self-centeredness. Think of a spectrum with "selfless" and "self-centered" on two opposite ends of it with self-care as a dot in the middle that represents balance between the two. Self-centeredness makes us self-seeking. Everything revolves around us and our needs and we have little empathy for others. We do things for others only in exchange for what it will bring us. Selflessness is the opposite in which we neglect ourselves and make ourselves a doormat for others. Self-centeredness and selflessness hold us back; self-care is the balance that propels us forward. Self-care gives us the confidence to move beyond ourselves and to extend ourselves by showing an interest in the thoughts and needs of others. It allows us to share and give to others and do kind deeds without the need for payoff or recognition. Human compassion and kindness come naturally with self-care.

At many spiritual retreat centers, participants often are assigned random duties to perform called selfless service. When I'm bent over that toilet bowl with brush in one hand and Comet cleanser in the other, scrubbing and flushing, just imagine all the thoughts that my ego screams at me! "How demeaning!" or "How was it that you got assigned the dirtiest job?" But the truth is that these kinds of humbling experiences put my ego in its place and prepare me to be more human on an equal plane with others. They prepare me to be more loving and compassionate and to receive these feelings from others.

One way you can rid yourself of self-seeking thoughts and take your mind off your troubles is to think of others' feelings, put others first sometimes, or perform an anonymous act of kindness or selfless service. Volunteering your services, helping a stranger, donating money for a worthy cause, teaching a class at church or synagogue all are ways of moving away from the self-centered side of the spectrum and toward the middle. In the words of John Ruskin, "When a man is wrapped up in himself, he makes a pretty small package." Once you have enough self-confidence and self-respect to perform selfless service for others, you will wrap yourself in a bigger, more bounteous and beautiful package that you can proudly carry through life.

Take Your Life More Lightly

Angels can fly because they take themselves lightly.
—G. K. Chesterton

Having spent a week camping at the ocean, a group of friends and I stopped at a Dairy Queen and sat around eating our ice cream and exchanging stories. One person told a story that was so funny that the group broke into uncontrollable laughter. The snickering and chuckling continued for well over ten minutes. As hard as we tried, we couldn't stop giggling. After fifteen minutes, we were no longer laughing at the joke, but at the fact that we couldn't stop laughing. Tears streamed down our cheeks. Our sides were splitting with pain. Some of us were running to the rest room. Our laughter became contagious. Other customers started laughing too. Employees peered from the back to see what all the ruckus was about. Before we knew it, they too were bent double laughing. At the time we left, the entire establishment was rollicking with side-splitting laughter. As we drove away, we left a small army of people holding their chests and wiping away tears. It was a memory and a feeling I will always cherish. The laughing made me feel better and more connected to life than I had ever remembered.

Some of us take life's challenges with grim, humorless determination and think it has to be all work and no play. We believe we must toil and sweat before we earn the right to have fun. We may even feel guilty laughing and smiling because we feel we don't deserve it. The truth is that a lighthearted and fun-filled life is everyone's birthright. A balanced life requires us to be as open to laughter and humor as we are to pain and sorrow.

Neuroscience confirms that laughter is good medicine. It makes us feel better and live longer. Biochemical research has shown that laughter activates the secretion of hormones that can make us happier. Endorphins, the body's own painkillers, help reduce physical pain. Humor and lightheartedness also can reduce stress, foster physical healing, and brighten your outlook, regardless of how grim your situation. Anger can kill us, and laughter can heal and sustain us. If you learn to have fun and think positively, your body will produce interleukins and interferons—powerful cancer-fighting chemicals.

In his book, *Headfirst*, Norman Cousins (1989) declares, "Scarcely anything that enters the mind doesn't find its way into the makeup of the body." We become the recipients of our own joy and elation or frustration or rage. Uplifting, light moods have positive physical effects, while dark moods have harmful physical effects on the body. When we are overly stressed, our brains send the message to the body through cortisol and adrenaline—stress hormones that can destroy the immune system. Under stress, epinephrine makes the heart beat fast and blood pressure rise which can lead to damaged arteries and heart attack. High stress and negative feelings such as frustration or depression also have been linked to chemical changes believed to produce certain cancerous cells. Positive thoughts and emotions, on the other hand, create body chemistry that has beneficial side effects, boosting the immune system. Laughter enhances the immune system by increasing the number of disease-fighting cells.

My friends on the Suwannee River have shown me how to lighten up and have fun. Whether we're cat fishing, exploring the river for alligators, or diving in the nearby Gulf for scallops, it seems we're always laughing. One of the funniest things they do is rate each boat or skier that passes by the dock. Five or six friends sitting shoulder to shoulder will sit on the dock with paper plates numbered one through ten in large print. As the boat passes, everyone raises their plate with a number on it. The reaction from the passersby is anything from high fives and hysterical laughter to the finger. Some "judges" even give zero or 1/2 ratings to the biggest, most expensive yachts, just to help them with their egos and give them a dose of humility.

Almost anything can be taken as an opportunity to lighten up. The potential for having fun and seeing the humorous side of life is all around you: the funny things children say, a joke someone tells, something silly you do. Your prescription for a happy and lengthy life is one or more big belly laughs per day.

Immerse Yourself In "Deep Play"

Deep play helps us feel balanced, creative, focused and at peace.

—Diane Ackerman

From the time I could hold a pencil, I spent hours alone in my room writing mystery stories. I loved it because the characters I created would do anything I wanted them to do. I got them into trouble and at the stroke of my pencil saved them from peril. I had full rein over characters who went wild in my vivid childhood imagination. Writing not only gave me a sense of control over my unwieldy life but also provided a sanctuary from all the seemingly inexplicable events that surrounded and threatened to engulf me. My pretend stories became plays that I'd make my neighborhood friends act out. I was not only the writer but also the director. We'd hang up old bedspreads for curtains and my front porch doubled as stage.

Today, writing still picks me up and carries me away into another sphere. Hours go by and it seems like minutes. It feels magical, comforting, and satisfying. Nothing is more fulfilling and joyous than constructing words to form sentences that express exactly what I want to say in just the right way. For me writing is what the author Diane Ackerman calls "deep play." Deep play is a form of rapture, created by an altered state, that brings you joy well-being, and inner calm. You can create this state through an activity or pastime that you are passionate about, something you can become so immersed in that you lose all track of time. For some people it's painting, sailing, gardening, tennis, woodworking, skiing, or running. For others it is wandering aimlessly in antique galleries, milling around attic sales, or browsing in bookstores—any activities in which your mind sidesteps reality.

My other favorite pastimes are tennis and traveling, especially to tropical rain forests—both of which take me deep into myself. I even tried my hand at acting which you may have read in an earlier section. But nothing absorbs me like writing. In her book, *Deep Play*, Ackerman (1999) stresses the importance of going deep into one pastime instead of shallowly into three or four. The deepness or immersion is key—an activity that so engulfs you that you lose track of time and feel blanketed in its refuge, comforted from the worries of everyday life.

Jamey creates deep play by working with his orchids. He describes his passion as Nirvana—an out-of-body experience much like meditation in which he is totally involved, self-contained, and at peace. He says that when he's working with the flowers that time stands still and that there are no outside sounds, only the sounds in front of him—digging, pulling, raking. He has a heightened awareness in which colors are more intense and objects he hadn't noticed before reveal themselves.

Some experts say deep play is a need as basic for healthy living as diet, rest, and exercise and that we need it to maintain proper balance in our lives. So making time for an enjoyable pastime can help you put and keep your life on an even keel. What you want to do is identify one thing—a hobby, recreation, or creative outlet—you really like or think you'd like that allows you self-expression. Try your hand at playing a musical instrument, composing poetry, cooking, playing organized sports, rock climbing, or working with clay. The play you choose can be something you're not even very good at, and it doesn't have to culminate in a tangible product. Sheer enjoyment from the process of self-involvement is what you want to aim for. It can be a group activity, such as an art class, or it can be an individual activity. There is no prescribed way to select your play activity. Just base your choice on what you enjoy and what suits your interests and schedule. Whatever you choose, explore it completely—on the surface, inside out, upside down, and rightside up—with all its nuances and complexities. Let the activity envelop you and burrow into the core of your soul. Sound dramatic? It is, but so are the results you'll enjoy.

Think with Your Heart

A mind all logic is like a knife all blade. It makes the hand bleed that uses it.

—Tagore

Doorbells chimed and phones rang off the hook. My coauthors and I had set up shop at my friend Carol's house in Columbia, South Carolina to decide which publisher to sign with for the first book we'd ever written. Five major publishers, eager to get our John Hancocks on the dotted line, pursued us. They wired flowers, sent candy and gifts, and delivered boxes of sample books for us to examine. Editors flew in from five different parts of the country. As we ushered one out the back door, we showed another through the front door. But after the dust settled, we couldn't come to a decision.

Wet behind the ears and overwhelmed, we struggled to make sense of the data and facts we'd gathered. All five publishing houses made good offers and all five produced good products. We were stymied. When they offered to fly me to meet the people behind the scenes, my co-authors instructed me to throw out logic (since that hadn't worked) and to use my heart as a barometer. Our game plan was to imagine that if we lived in the publishing house and the employees were our families, which one would we choose? Suddenly it became easy. Going with our hearts instead of our heads was how we made our decision, and we never regretted it.

Try driving from California to New York without a road map. Try sailing unfamiliar Caribbean seas without a compass. Try flying an airplane without proper equipment. When we're going somewhere, we need proper guidance to get there. Without help to keep us on track, we're likely to end up someplace we don't want to be. The mind is our vehicle in life, but the heart is our compass. The great minds in history have said it, but perhaps none so eloquently as Antoine de Saint-Exupery: "It is only with the heart that one can see rightly; what is essential is invisible to the eye."

Too much reason can confuse us and make us indecisive. For example, if you've been invited to a farewell party for a colleague and you're racking your brain, debating on whether or not to go, you can probably think of a hundred reasons you "should" or "shouldn't" go: "I already gave my RSVP; I told everyone I'd be there; I helped plan the party and it can't go on without me; I need to be there just in case no one else shows." On the other hand, "I never liked the guy; I already did my part by planning the party; I'm entitled to last-minute changes in plans, just like anyone else; I could use that time to do some of the other things that are on my plate." And on and on. When this type of inner dialogue happens with big or small decisions, the key is to get out of your head and go straight to your feelings, because when the head and heart conflict, your heart rarely leads you astray. Ask yourself what *you* really want or need in regard to the decision. You can even close your eyes and contemplate in your heart of hearts what direction to take. Reframe the decision you have to make by asking, "Will it bring me happiness?" This question will give you greater clarity and make your choices easier. When I let myself really listen with my heart instead of my head, my intuitive self speaks to me and guides me.

Our intuition sends us messages that are as essential to our happiness and that deserve as much attention as our thoughts. When you take a wrong turn or get lost but are willing to heed the message, your intuitive self can put you back on track. Listening with your heart instead of your head from time to time can keep you on your path and give you the confidence and peace of mind that you're making the right decision or headed in the right direction.

It's important to listen to the heart when it says "go" or "stop" and "be careful" or "take it easy." Whether you're making career choices, deciding about important relationships, or facing any other personal options, the answers you seek will come to you from within when you put yourself under the proper conditions. Whatever important life decisions you face, it's important to look at your choices logically. But the complimentary approach you can use is to close your eyes, quiet your mind, and listen to what your heart says. Listening with your heart and less with your head can bring you the assurance and calm you've been seeking.

Stop Postponing Your Life

Gather ye rosebuds while ye may, Old Time is still a-flying, and this same flower that smiles today, tomorrow will be dying.

—Robert Herrick

I am learning to live my life each day so that if someone were to ask me, "If you had your life to live over, what would you change?" My answer would be, "Not one single thing!" Of course, it's not an easy thing to do, but I feel like it's an admirable goal to keep striving for. Amid all the hustle and bustle and the daily grind, I make it a point to try to "go for the gusto." Unfortunately, though, for many of us life is what happens while we're making other plans. And the fun and joy keep slipping through our fingers.

Every time I go to my place on the Suwannee River, I'm reminded of Henry Miller's comment that "Life, as it is called, is for most of us one long postponement." Life on the Suwannee is sweeter, simpler, and richer. Butterflies play tag in the sunlight, mullet turn somersaults midair before splashing their declaration of independence, and the warm river water beckons on balmy summer nights. Most evenings a gathering of river dwellers sits around a blazing campfire and talks about life, offering wisdom I need to hear. One evening in particular stands out in my mind.

One man told us how he left his insurance business to realize a lifelong dream of being a sea captain in the Gulf. He shared tales of wealthy businessmen twice his age lamenting that they postponed their dreams to make money. And now it was too late for them to do anything about it. Another man spoke of an uncle who spent his entire life sacrificing and saving for retirement and then dropped dead the day before the big event. A woman mentioned a co-worker who kept swearing she'd quit work to be with her small children. But money to buy more things convinced her to postpone her departure, and before she knew it, her kids were fully grown. She had missed their first words, those first steps, and even their first recitals. She described it as "the toothpaste was out of the tube—there's no putting it back."

Carpe diem is Latin for "seize the day." It cautions us to live in the "now," because the present is the most important time we have. It reminds us to live our lives fully, not worrying about what went wrong or about what might go wrong. As long as we live in the future or dwell in the past, we miss the present. Hugh Prather said, "Every moment that I am centered in the future, I suffer a temporary loss of life." If you think of your own mortality and how fleeting life is, what comes to mind that needs attention? If you had your life to live over, what would you do differently? An anonymous writer answered that question this way: " If I had my life to live over, I would have talked less and listened more. I would have invited friends over even though the carpet was stained and the sofa was faded. I would have burned the candle sculpted like a rose before it melted in storage. I would have gone to bed when I was sick instead of worrying that the earth would go into a holding pattern if I missed work. There would have been more 'I love you,' more 'I am sorry.'"

Think of three of your favorite things you like to do that bring you joy. You might list them in your head or write them down. Now think of the last time you did each one. Was it a day ago, a week ago, a month ago, or years ago? What does this information tell you about how you're living your life? Did you have trouble even thinking of three favorite things? Are you doing the things you want to do in your life? Or are you living your life for everybody else? If so, take charge and start doing what you really want to do. Have more lifelines than deadlines. Have more health days than sick days. Pay more attention to what goes right instead of what goes wrong. Have more joy and more fun.

You're making choices every moment of your life, and you won't come this way again. Once you are really living your life fully, as if each day were your last, you won't have to ask yourself these kinds of questions anymore. And you won't give a second thought to John Greenleaf Whittier's famous warning: "For of all sad words of tongue or pen, the saddest are these: 'It might have been!'"

126

7

Develop Healthy Relationships

Relationships are only as good as the people engaging in them.

—Donald Ardell

Celebrate the Good Fortunes of Others

Envy comes from people's ignorance of, or lack of belief in, their own gifts.

—Jean Vanier

I have a friend who feels cheated when she sees good things happen to other people. I'm amazed at how a stroke of luck for someone else can be a slap in the face for her. She constantly complains about a coworker whom she calls a braggart and who makes her feel "inept." She says that the coworker is always "bragging" about how great his life is and about the accomplishments of his children. "I don't want to hear all that stuff," my friend whines. "It just makes me feel like my life's nothing."

Recently, I got a good deal on a small getaway shack on the Suwannee River in Florida. I was very excited about having this quiet little retreat and I wanted to share my happiness with my friend. But after I told her, I was sorry I did. An ugly frown came over her face, as if she were physically ill. She said, "Why do you always have the good luck? How come it always has to be you? Why couldn't it be me?" I started to tell her to take two aspirin, go to bed, and call the doctor in the morning. But she stamped her foot and snorted, as if she had caught herself, "Oh I'm happy for you!" Yet her tone didn't match her words.

Sometimes the good fortunes of others are reminders of our own unhappiness. How do you react when a friend strikes it rich? A coworker gets a big promotion? A neighbor inherits a lot of money? A family member takes a trip around the world? Do you feel jealous or bitter? Do you wish that it had been you? Do you see their good fortunes as your loss? Do you feel like you have to "keep up with the Joneses"? Most of us at one time or another have silently, if not openly, envied the successes of our friends. You might ask, "Why in the world would I be excited about someone else's happiness when it doesn't make my life better?" That's a good question to which there are some very good answers.

Let's connect the dots here. First of all, my friend's reaction was an example of someone who is blind to her own gifts and who is displeased with the choices she has made in her own life. It was the reaction of someone who compares her life to others and comes up empty-handed. When you constantly compare your lot to friends, coworkers, or neighbors and feel cheated, you automatically get a false sense of emptiness. This outlook can throw you into a pit of despair and make you feel as if others have it all and you have nothing. This kind of comparison is another example of your mind stunting your growth. Focusing on what others have can keep you from seeing your own riches and can also stop you form realizing that you have some other blessings that they don't. Yours are just different from theirs.

Envy is a selfish act that can only increase your feelings of poverty. In order to rejoice in the good fortunes of others, you have to learn to get outside of yourself and to care about them. The key is to start to appreciate your own gifts and give thanks for what you have instead of focusing on others' blessings. Rejoice in your uniqueness and talents. Peace of mind comes from being grateful for what you have—not from wanting what others have—and from taking the necessary action to create other choices for yourself if you are dissatisfied with your life.

But the best reason I can give you for celebrating other people's prosperity is that when you genuinely share in someone else's good fortune, it makes you feel good too. When you participate in the joy, you feel the joy! When you pound a table, stamp your foot, or harbor resentments, it makes you feel bad. Wouldn't you rather feel good than bad? Feeling envy or resentment won't change things, anyway. So when good things happen to others, why not become part of the celebration, choose joy over disappointment, and feel the good feelings? When you experience the joy of others and hold it in your heart, a strange thing happens. You suddenly have good fortune too, because you're sharing in the feelings instead of selfishly separating yourself by hoarding bitterness.

Here's a challenge for you: the next time something good happens to someone close to you, make a special effort to join in their happiness, share in their feelings, and notice how much better it makes *you* feel, too.

Keep Important Relationships Alive

Love doesn't just sit there like a stone; it has to be made, like bread, remade all the time, made new.

—Ursula K. LeGuin

The wife of a corporate head said that upon arriving home from the office, her husband ignores her and walks straight to his study where he checks his fax and e-mail, opens his briefcase, then goes straight upstairs to lay out the clean shirt, pants, tie, and jacket for the next morning.

Feel sympathy for her? Not so fast. She says she is busy cooking dinner, talking on her cell phone to the employees at work, chauffeuring the kids to and from their after-school activities, getting them ready for bed, and completing sales reports that her supervisor expects the next day.

It's not unusual for the typical millennium couple to find that their relationship is stale from neglect. After a full day at the office, more couples are spending evenings cooking meals, talking business, attending to children, troubleshooting, and in some cases preparing work for the next day. The relationships can be damaged when business relationships replace intimate relationships: discussing financial concerns instead of feelings; hassles of the job instead of problems in the relationship; headaches with the kids instead of breakdown in their own communication.

Eventually these overworked relationships start to show the same signs of neglect and stress that an overworked individual does: irritability, tension, exhaustion, and resentment. Sometimes couples shut down completely and don't talk at all. Over time, some couples associate their relationships only with problems and troubleshooting. As communication starts to feel like another demand, both parties may unwittingly look for ways to escape closeness with one another—as when television or late-night work becomes a replacement for companionship or when children become an emotional replacement for the intimate partner. One of the biggest problems I see during marriage therapy is when the parental bond gets stronger than the marital bond. When this happens, the relationship is in trouble.

Relationships are fluid, growing entities with a life of their own. They must have attention to stay vital. If you purchase a beautiful plant, set it in a dark corner and return in a few months, it would be dead. You don't expect plants to thrive without nourishment, water, and light. In the same way undernourished relationships wither away without proper attention. Another way to think about your intimate relationship is to think of it as a bank account, which I asked you to do about yourself in an earlier passage. As with any bank account, relationships require periodic deposits to stay solvent—affectionate touch, heart-to-heart talks, encouragement, forgiveness, understanding, compassion. These deposits offset the withdrawals that naturally occur in any relationship—demands, stress, criticism, broken promises, blame, disagreements, and misunderstandings.

You can start to nurture your relationship by drawing the line about the amount of time you spend working with your intimate partner, talking about work, or discussing family business or scheduling. You can tailor this boundary around your unique schedules and lifestyles. One possibility is to eliminate work after a set evening hour and to carve out a set time weekday evenings (without television) for personal conversations about nonwork-related matters. Mealtime is a great time to put these boundaries in place; another possibility is to set aside the time immediately after your partner arrives home or to establish a special date night (without children) where you share dinner or another activity together. You can make sure you have healthy pastimes that you share as a couple such as tennis, golf, or just walking. Or you can make a special effort to keep your romance alive by creating special moments at home or at a special restaurant or by giving your love partner special reminders that say "I love you."

Whatever course of action you take, the key to revitalizing your relationship is taking time out for maintaining your emotional connection and support through the sea of daily work, chores, commitments, and miscommunication. It's good economics to ask yourself each day what you've deposited into your relationship. If you make just one deposit a day, you'll get back a thousand fold what you've put into it.

Avoid Relationships Where You're Joined at the Hip

Care is no cure, but rather corrosive, for things that are not to be remedied.
—William Shakespeare

Before Nora took her first vacation in two years to visit her sister, she cooked, labeled, and froze meals for her family. She arranged notes around the house to help her husband and kids limp through daily routines during her two-day absence. She washed all their clothes, cleaned the house from top to bottom, and arranged her children's outfits and carpool. She spent her time away from home worrying that her family could not manage without her. She found it impossible to have a good time and be emotionally present with her sister because she felt guilty for being away. When she returned home and discovered that her family had done great without her, Nora felt jealous and unappreciated, even angry.

This story begs the question, "Whose needs are being met here? Nora's? Or her family's?" I'm certainly not against doing good deeds and helping people out, but sometimes we have to ask ourselves what our motives are. Nora's need for her family to be unable to function without her goes over the line of healthy caring and into the realm of unhealthy dependence. Nora's strength was being gained at the expense of her family's weakness.

Nora and her family might as well be joined at the hip. Sometimes being overly helpful becomes the ego's way of feeding off the needs of others so that we can feel needed. The spiritual teacher Ram Dass said, "If you need to be helpful, you'll look for someone to be helpless." Keeping others helpless so that we can be helpful is disrespectful and damaging to all parties involved whether at home, work, or play. Consider the people you know who are overly committed: the person who ends up running most of the carpools in the neighborhood; the parent who joins every committee at school because "If I don't, who will?"; the worker who feels taken advantage of because coworkers don't do their part; the friend who gives advice and gets angry when it's not taken; the spouse who always does for the partner but doesn't feel that it gets reciprocated. Do any of these people sound like you?

Carried too far, the helper robs the helped of the ability to manage their own lives. And the helper counts on the helped to be dependent, because that's where the ego gains its worth. When we are overly focused on taking care of someone else, we don't have to think about ourselves, our needs, our problems. Nora was finally able to break through her ego needs and learn to be a genuine helpmate to family and friends. She realized that she had been really caring for herself, giving to others what *she* wanted, and secretly hoping they would need and appreciate her for being such a loving and caring person.

Sylvia's and Lisa's husbands bowl together on Thursday nights. Lisa enjoys the time away from her husband because it gives her a chance to do things she enjoys doing alone. But Sylvia is jealous of bowling and gets upset when her husband bowls without her because, she says, "He'd rather be with his friends than me." The family is inseparable. When one member goes to Wal-Mart, the whole family has to go. Sylvia and her family might as well be joined at the hip.

If you do catch yourself in a dependent relationship, I suggest that you explore ways of caring for and nurturing yourself. Begin to realize that while helping does feel good, finding someone to rescue or fix is not what defines your worth. Then find other healthier activities and goals that can fill any emptiness you might feel and give you the self-worth you've been seeking. I wouldn't go so far as to recommend that you not be helpful to others. But when you help others, make sure that your helping results in others' growing ability to stand on their own two feet. Give only as much help as is really needed—allowing, encouraging, and perhaps teaching others to be self-reliant. With children, this may consist of showing them how to do tasks like cleaning up their rooms, folding laundry, or tying their shoes instead of doing it for them. With friends it may be listening and supporting instead of offering advice and occasionally saying no when asked for help. With intimate partners it may be feeling as good when you're apart as when you're together. Because then you know you're both whole.

Don't Hold Too Tightly to the Ones You Love

Love is the child of freedom, never that of domination.

—Erich Fromm

Once I had a patient, Jim, who came to counseling because he was obsessed with the belief that his wife was going to cheat on him. The fear so controlled him that he dominated his wife's every move. At parties he wouldn't let her out of his sight. He followed her to get drinks and even to the rest room where he waited outside for her. He sent her flowers and cards every day and told her he loved her every hour on the hour. Can you imagine how nerve-racking it would be to have someone hovering over you and anticipating your every move? It was a maddening experience for the wife and an agonizing burden for the husband.

The paradox is that those of us who fear abandonment often help create it by holding on too tightly to the ones we love and strangling the life out of the relationship. After a while, loved ones can't take the stress of the confinement anymore and they leave. This is exactly what almost happened with the couple above.

So what do you do about the fear of abandonment? Start with finding out where your fear comes from. The answers almost always lie in the past. Tears streaming down his cheeks, Jim told me of an incident when, as an excited nine-year-old, he rushed home to share his good grades with his mother. As he barged through her bedroom door, his confused eyes saw her in bed with the preacher. She leapt from her bed and began to beat and scold him for intruding into her bedroom. His enthusiasm was squashed and, even more painful, his trust in close loved ones was permanently fractured. Before meeting his wife, every woman he loved had cheated on him. Jim's frame of reference told him that you can't trust women, and this was the belief he imposed on his wife, regardless of the fact that she was a virgin when he met her and had never even thought about cheating on him.

I suggested to him that it wasn't fair to blame his wife for what his mother and his girlfriends had done in his youth. The realization that it wasn't his wife's fault helped Jim see her differently and change his behavior accordingly. It helped him relax in the marriage, giving the relationship a feeling of freedom that helped his wife want to be closer to him instead of pushing him away.

A loving relationship is built on freedom, not domination. Strong relationships are based on trust and freedom; weak relationships are based on fear, which leads to imposed authority and domination. If you have nagging thoughts that, "He's going to leave me" or "She's going to find someone else," chances are that a past experience is causing these thoughts—a past experience that probably has nothing to do with your present ones. Your insecurity about being abandoned could be causing you to collect evidence that the people you love now are also planning to leave you, even if this "evidence" actually means something entirely different. Your fear can make you misread the most innocent words and actions of your loved ones, putting a heavy burden on your relationships. These unfounded fears can put distance between you and your beloved, keeping you from being close. When you remind yourself that these are only *thoughts* that do not fit with the real events of your life, you can stop acting on them and see your loved one for who he or she really is.

Honor Yourself as Much as You Honor Your Children

Insanity is hereditary — you can get it from your children.

—Sam Levenson

A mound of homemade biscuits, golden fried chicken, and fluffy mashed potatoes spread on a table that seemed to go on for miles. That's how Art recalls his boyhood memory of Sunday dinners in the South. In those days children sat at one end of the table, and adults helped themselves first to the white meat of the chicken. By the time the chicken platter reached the other end of the table, only dark meat was left for Art and the other youngsters. But they didn't care. And they never thought of complaining or questioning the tradition. That was just the way things were back then. Grown-ups were first and children, although loved and cared for, were second, and there was a good feeling about that.

Fast forward to the millennium. At large family gatherings Art and his wife sit at one end of the table and their children and cousins at the opposite end. The children get their hands on the white meat first. By the time the platter of chicken gets to the adult end of the table, Art is left with only dark meat. My, how times have changed. But he doesn't mind, because he's giving them what he never got. Or is he?

What's wrong with this picture? You might see it as a metaphor for how well-intended grown ups overindulge today's kids, taking second seat to them in the name of love. This role-reversal puts children in the driver's seat and adults in the back, along for the ride. Sound scary? Here's an everyday example of what I'm talking about. Mildred complained that her fourteen-year-old daughter sequesters herself in her room with her door locked, playing heavy metal music and coming out only to eat. Mildred casually mentioned to me that her daughter emerged over the weekend and told her she was going to her friend Jenny's to spend the night. I asked Mildred if her daughter "told" her or "asked" her.

Mildred cocked her head and, as if having an epiphany, said "She *told* me, and I went right along with it."

The problem with overindulgence is that it gives children authority that they are emotionally and mentally ill-equipped to handle. Too much control feels scary to them, even if they don't or can't say so. And the worst part is that it turns them into narcissistic, insecure, selfish, and demanding youngsters who have complete disregard for others.

The generational line between adulthood and childhood has all but been erased. It's important for grown-ups to put that line back in place—the invisible line with adults above it and children below it that lets kids know, "I'm the adult; you're the child." That line defines the roles, provides insulation and security to kids and makes them feel safe and cared for. Of course, children will buck the line—that's what they're supposed to do. And when that happens, you want to ship the kids off to relatives and disappear into a federal witness protection program, but you hold the line firmly in place. That's what adults are supposed to do.

"Parenting" is an action verb, not just a noun. So ask yourself, "Am I just wearing the title? Or am I putting it into action with my child?" If you've been too lax, start drawing the line, learn to say "no," and "I love you" in the same sentence, and let your child know who's in charge. Remind yourself you're not taking anything away from them; you're giving them something: insulation, security, and the message, "I love and care about you." Remember, what children resent you for now, they'll thank you for someday.

Don't Let Anyone Rent Space in Your Head

It is tragic how few people ever possess their souls before they die; most people are other people. Their thoughts are someone else's opinions, their lives a mimicry, their passions a quotation.

—Oscar Wilde

When Diane was a child, her dad gave her a dollar every time she read *How to Win Friends and Influence People*, and she really internalized that book. She says it taught her the people-pleasing stuff—tuning in to others and making them feel important. Diane realized that underneath all that kind manipulation was the need to control how others felt about her. That was how she learned to feel okay about herself. Problem was she felt it was more important for other people to like her than for her to like herself. So she learned to gain approval through charm and people pleasing while privately feeling shortchanged.

Today Diane still struggles with whether it's okay for her to be different from others. She worries about what people think if she doesn't meet their standards or do things the way they do. This fear of being different is based on her insecurity that she might not be okay if others don't agree or approve. Being accepted and understood has been one of her coping devices: being a good girl, a good daughter, doing all the things she's supposed to do. If she wanted Chinese and you wanted Mexican, she was willing to give up her wants. If you needed her to help you paint your apartment on her only day off, she would accommodate you. It kills her to be a disappointment to someone or to let them down. She has gone to such lengths to please others that she has forgotten who *she* is and what she needs for herself.

Winston Churchill once said, "An appeaser is one who feeds a crocodile—hoping it will eat him last." Approval seekers think that doing "right," which is often doing what others want, is more important than being who you really are. They become chameleons, changing colors to fit in with whomever they are with at the moment, molding their attitudes, emotions, and behaviors around the wishes of everybody else. Somewhere in their pursuit to measure up outwardly, they lose touch with who they are on the inside, because the views of others occupy that space.

Have you sold out to the approval of others? Have you leased your heart and soul to loved ones, friends, or acquaintances, allowing them to rent space in your head? When you trim yourself to suit everybody else, you whittle yourself away until there's nothing left of you. Your mind is *your* place. Nobody has squatter's rights in your head unless you give it, and that's a choice you make every second of the day. Living your life by what others think puts them, instead of you, in charge of your life. When your personality changes with the wind, you lose your self-respect. And if you don't know your mind and take a stand for what you believe, you'll lose the respect of the people around you.

Overcoming people pleasing allows you to live your life according to what's right for you, not anyone else. You can accomplish this by standing firm about who you are and what you believe in. You will earn the respect of others, but more importantly, you'll have your own self-respect first. Part of taking charge of your life is letting go of other people's opinions, forming your own, and living your life to suit yourself. The philosopher Epictetus said it best: "We are not injured by the opinions of others but by our own belief that their opinions are important."

I made a pact with myself a long time ago to stop feeding the alligator of appeasement and to start possessing my own soul. What about you? Is your life guided by the wishes and whims of others? Do you blame yourself because of something someone else does that you really cannot control? Is there someone in your life whose words or deeds hook you into believing you caused them? If you said yes to any of these questions, ask yourself what course of action you can take to get your life back. Start carving out *your* opinions, *your* life, *your* passions, and start possessing *your* soul. When you do, no one else will be able to rent space in your head again.

Don't Micromanage Relationships

A controller doesn't trust his/her ability to live through the pain and chaos of life. There is no life without pain just as there is no art without submitting to chaos.

—Rita Mae Brown

I'm the kind of person who hits the ground running, takes control of a task, ends up doing all the work, and then complains that nobody helped—whether it's doing housework, coordinating social events with friends, or collaborating on a work assignment. Once on a project with my friend Nancy, I felt like I had done the majority of the work. Not because she didn't do her part, but because I didn't give her a chance to do more. She said something to me that opened my eyes and stuck with me: "You know, when one person *overfunctions* in a relationship, the other automatically *underfunctions*." She's right. It's like a formula. And the other thing I've noticed is that when one party underfunctions, the other feels resentful that they have to pick up the slack, even though they helped create it. If something goes wrong, the overfunctioning party gets blamed. You can apply this formula in work projects, friendships, or in family interactions.

I knew a woman named Kim who micromanaged a brittle relationship between her husband and his mother. The problem was that Kim felt she was always in the middle. One day Kim orchestrated a Christmas luncheon at her mother-in-law's house. Although her husband and children begrudgingly went along, Kim believed it was her obligation as good wife to keep peace in the family. At the end of the long day when Kim announced it was time to go, the mother-in-law snapped, "Shut up and sit down! Can't you see everybody's having a good time? Why are you always running the show?" Kim was hurt and resentful. She had spent most of her marriage trying to hold the family together, then getting smacked in the face for her efforts.

Kim fits the overfunctioning formula. She did both her share and her husband's, which automatically reduced his part. So naturally Kim got the mother-in-law's wrath, because the formula demands that the one playing center stage catches the heat when things go wrong. It also means that the person who overfunctions often ends up feeling bitter and unappreciated.

If you ever find yourself caught as third party in a tense triangle, the best advice is to step out of the middle. Even better advice is to not let yourself get put there in the first place, if you can help it. Whether it's getting caught between a demanding spouse and defiant children, two unhappy parents, two feuding friends, two competing colleagues, or between your spouse and their parent, third party in a triangle is a dangerous place to be. You end up catching the grief while the two other parties fail to work out their problems, because you're in the way. The good news is that Kim learned a two-word lesson: "Step aside." She vowed after that disastrous holiday luncheon to stay out of the middle of other people's relationships and let them work out their differences.

The times that I've caught myself overfunctioning in relationships, I usually had good intentions of wanting people I love to get along. Or in worrying over someone's safety, I hovered over them or overly directed them. Then it dawned on me when I looked at the situation from their point of view that it didn't feel like love and caring to them. It felt more like I was trying to control them.

The key here is to evaluate your own share of control in your relationships. Ask yourself, "Am I too controlling? Do I micromanage people around me? Do I try to patch relationships that are not my concern? Do I take more than my share of responsibility in work, family, or social interactions?"

If you say yes to any of these questions, you can learn to let go of some of the control. One strategy that works is to remind yourself to "get out of the way" when you get triangled between two people, or to "let go" when you're too controlling of others. You may be surprised at how much better you will feel if you learn to lovingly release control and let others work out their own problems. If you want to quit being a control freak, you can let everyone around you be responsible for their part and take only your share. When you do this, you'll have more energy to devote to managing your own life.

Love Your Partner's Virtues and Vices

Vices are sometimes only virtues carried to excess.

—Charles Dickens

I'll never forget the day we met. Atlanta. 1970. Bell bottoms, peace symbols, and shoulder-length hair were the rage. After thirty years what I still remember most about my mate are those beautiful green eyes. That witty, devil-may-care arrogance. That fun-loving, exciting and spur-of-the-moment zest for life. It's funny how, after only five years, that carefree, playful, free spirit I had met suddenly transformed into an indifferent, unreliable, disorganized, and irresponsible slob.

Most of us are swept off our feet when we first meet the love of our life. We swoon. Our hearts leap. And their virtues naturally stand out from their vices. Then after a few years into the relationship we start to see the flipside of the coin: all the things that bug us. We say things like, "Boy, has she changed!" or "He's not the same man I married." But the truth is that she hasn't changed, and yes, he's *exactly* the same man you married. You're just seeing the other side. The things that cause problems for us in relationships are the flipside of the things that originally attracted us. Your partner's vices are really just virtues carried to excess. Think about it this way: Virtues contain vices. Strength contains willfulness, stability contains control, spontaneity contains abandon. You're getting a package deal. When the virtues get carried to excess, you get vices.

But don't feel alone. I interviewed my partner for this section and here's how I looked at our first encounter: "in charge, stable, feet on the ground, solid, serious." And here's how I looked after five years together: "controlling, rigid, uptight, and grumpy." Here's why: In every relationship one party is a *rock* and one is a *bird*. Rocks play their hands close to their chests, keep their feet planted firmly on the ground, are organized, logical, and usually have things under control. Birds will always show you their hand. They could care less about order and organization, and fly all around. They are playful, spontaneous, flexible, and flow with the moment. They are more creative and intuitive than rocks.

One style is not better or more right than the other. The bird and rock are just different, and both play important roles in the relationship. The rock provides the stability and the bird provides the levity—both of which are necessary ingredients to make a balanced match. Two rocks would sink from the intensity of the relationship and there would be no lightness. Two birds would fly off into the wild blue yonder, and nobody would be taking care of business. So, believe it or not, the rock and bird are a union made in heaven, even though it may not sound like it.

The rock tackles problems systematically by looking for the logical steps. The bird looks at things holistically not at the details. These differences can be sources of major conflict in long-term relationships. But they don't have to be. If you're willing to see the value in you partner's style—instead of thinking your way is right or better than your partner's, you'll notice a big difference in how you feel. And if you're willing to look for the virtues contained in your partner's vices—and to round out yourself by incorporating some of those virtues into yourself, you'll add a big plus to your relationship.

I challenge you to look at your love differently today. Start to think of him or her as your mirror opposite—the flipside of yourself that you never developed. After all, that's why opposites attract. Then see if you can discover the virtues in your partner's vices, and make a mental list of what you find. Next, think about who's the rock and bird in your intimate relationship. If you start to look at these differences as a plus, instead of a minus, you can use them to create balance in your relationship.

If you start to see these polar opposites as traits that can complete you and make you more well rounded, you'll be surprised at how much more you'll appreciate your relationship and how much more harmonious it will be.

See Your Endings as Beginnings in Disguise

What we call the beginning is often the end. And to make an end is to make a beginning. The end is where we start from.

—T.S. Eliot

The biggest challenge my family ever experienced came when my nephew was brutally murdered at the age of thirty-nine. A shining light had been darkened, a gentle voice had been silenced, giving us all a gnawing feeling of irretrievable loss. The shock and horror led us to hope there had been a mistake. Maybe if we hoped hard enough and waited long enough, he would walk through the door and back into our arms. Maybe if we kept our eyes open and ever vigilant we'd see his familiar shadow moving toward us on a crowded street or in a busy shopping mall. But no. The grieving had to begin. We had to acknowledge the ending and finally say good-bye.

Sometimes it is difficult to see that, just as the Phoenix rises from the ashes, we are always ending *and* beginning, all at the same time. Saying good-bye. Completing a class. New Year's Eve. Endings often fill us with grief because the loss overshadows the gain. Of course, endings can be sad and nostalgic, but they also have a bright side. On New Year's Eve you can have nostalgia about the past twelve months *and* enthusiastically make resolutions for the upcoming year. The end of summer shepherds in the beginning of fall. The ending of this book brings with it an opportunity for you to begin practicing principles contained here or even a chance to re-read portions that you found meaningful.

So far, grief continues to overshadow my struggle to find the beginning in the tragic loss of my nephew. I have dedicated this book to him, and that feels like a beginning for me. Perhaps, too, it's in the life-insurance policy that became a college trust-fund for his nieces and nephews. Perhaps it's the compassionate and respectful ways he treated others, inviting us to do the same. Perhaps it's all the lives he touched with his unconditional love and the challenge he left for each of us to develop our own potential to love in tribute to him. Perhaps it's *all* these things and more. Although the beginning his loss provides remains unclear, I have confidence that, even when we can't see or understand it immediately, there's always a beginning disguised in every ending.

The Dalai Lama says that the purpose of life is to seek happiness and that the key to finding it is to develop the capacity to see a given situation from a variety of perspectives. I believe him. This message has been taught for centuries by philosophers and spiritual leaders, and more recently rediscovered by psychotherapists and management consultants. It is a fundamental truth that has endured throughout the ages. Of all the readings in this book, this one contains the simplest and most profound message and the most difficult to carry out: When you can see a given situation from more than one viewpoint, your inner strength becomes greater than your outer strength and thus rules in every situation.

What you want to start to do is to feel sadness or nostalgia over a loss without staying stuck there, recognizing that out of that ending, something is being born. The key is to pinpoint what is starting anew from the endings in your life. Make a conscious effort to acknowledge and grieve the ending while simultaneously embracing whatever new is starting in your life.

As I mentioned at the beginning of this book, my experience at the Buddhist retreat center was both a beginning and an ending for me. Reading back over the passages I've written, it struck me how often I wrote about getting angry, frustrated, and stressed out—attributes that have occupied the greater part of my life. There's an old saying that you teach what you need to learn. In a way writing this book has been both a beginning and an ending for me, because it has carried me further on my path to self-understanding. It is also my hope that it takes you far on yours. In the words of T. S. Eliot, "We shall not cease from exploration, and the end of all of our exploring will be to arrive where we started and know the place for the first time."

References and Further Readings

Ackerman, Diane. 1999. *Deep Play*. New York: Random House.

Carter-Scott, Cherie. 1998. *If Life Is a Game, These Are the Rules*. New York: Broadway Books.

DeMello, Anthony. 1978. *Sadhana: A Way to God*. New York: Doubleday. Used by permission of Doubleday, a division of Random House, Inc.

His Holiness the Dalai Lama and Howard Cutler. 1998. *The Art of Happiness: A Handbook for Living*. New York: Penguin Books.

Houff, William H. 1989. *Infinity in Your Hand*. Spokane: Melior Publications. Used with the author's permission.

Kabat-Zinn, Jon. 1994. *Wherever You Go, There You Are*. New York: Hyperion.

Lama Surya Das. 1997. *Awakening the Buddha Within: Tibetan Wisdom for the Western World*. New York: Broadway Books.

Nelson, Portia. 1980. "Autobiography in Five Short Chapters." In *There's a Hole in My Sidewalk*. New York: Popular Library Edition.

Powell, John. 1969. *Why Am I Afraid to Tell You Who I Am?* Chicago, Ill.: Argus Communications.

Robinson, Bryan. 1991. *Heal Your Self-Esteem*. Deerfield Beach, FL: Health Communications.

———. 1998. *Chained to the Desk: A Guidebook for Workaholics, Their Partners and Children and the Clinicians Who Treat Them*. New York: NYU Press.

Seyle, Hans. 1956. *The Stress of Life*. New York: McGraw-Hill.

Siegel, Bernie. 1986. *Love, Medicine and Miracles*. New York: Harper and Row.

Williamson, Marianne. 1993. *A Return to Love*. New York: HarperCollins.

Zukav, Gary. 1989. *The Seat of the Soul*. New York: Simon & Schuster.

More New Harbinger Titles

THE SELF-ESTEEM COMPANION

Step-by-step instructions for over 60 simple exercises to help you unmask a punishing inner critic and begin to celebrate your personal strengths.

Item SECO $10.95

THE DAILY RELAXER

Simple, tension-relieving exercises that you can learn in less than ten minutes and practice with positive results right away.

Item DALY Paperback, $12.95

CLAIMING YOUR CREATIVE SELF

The inspiring stories of thirteen women who were able to keep in touch with their own creative spirit opens the door to new definitions of creativity, and to the kinds of transforming ideas that will change your life.

Item CYCS $15.95

SIX KEYS TO CREATING THE LIFE YOU DESIRE

Helps you learn how to build a sense of trust, acknowledge your accomplishments, stop comparing yourself to others, achieve closeness, stop doubting your competence, and identify a core purpose that will let you follow through on your dreams.

Item KEY6 $19.95

BEING, BELONGING, DOING

Balancing Your Three Greatest Needs

This inspiring new book by therapist Ron Potter-Efron invites us to reevaluate our priorities and explore practical ways of keeping the components of our lives integrated and in balance.

Item BBD Paperback, $10.95

Call **toll-free 1-800-748-6273** to order. Have your Visa or Mastercard number ready. Or send a check for the titles you want to New Harbinger Publications, 5674 Shattuck Avenue, Oakland, CA 94609. Include $3.80 for the first book and 75¢ for each additional book to cover shipping and handling. (California residents please include appropriate sales tax.) Allow four to six weeks for delivery.

Prices subject to change without notice.

Some Other New Harbinger Self-Help Titles

Virtual Addiction, $12.95
After the Breakup, $13.95
Why Can't I Be the Parent I Want to Be?, $12.95
The Secret Message of Shame, $13.95
The OCD Workbook, $18.95
Tapping Your Inner Strength, $13.95
Binge No More, $14.95
When to Forgive, $12.95
Practical Dreaming, $12.95
Healthy Baby, Toxic World, $15.95
Making Hope Happen, $14.95
I'll Take Care of You, $12.95
Survivor Guilt, $14.95
Children Changed by Trauma, $13.95
Understanding Your Child's Sexual Behavior, $12.95
The Self-Esteem Companion, $10.95
The Gay and Lesbian Self-Esteem Book, $13.95
Making the Big Move, $13.95
How to Survive and Thrive in an Empty Nest, $13.95
Living Well with a Hidden Disability, $15.95
Overcoming Repetitive Motion Injuries the Rossiter Way, $15.95
What to Tell the Kids About Your Divorce, $13.95
The Divorce Book, Second Edition, $15.95
Claiming Your Creative Self: True Stories from the Everyday Lives of Women, $15.95
Six Keys to Creating the Life You Desire, $19.95
Taking Control of TMJ, $13.95
What You Need to Know About Alzheimer's, $15.95
Winning Against Relapse: A Workbook of Action Plans for Recurring Health and Emotional Problems, $14.95
Facing 30: Women Talk About Constructing a Real Life and Other Scary Rites of Passage, $12.95
The Worry Control Workbook, $15.95
Wanting What You Have: A Self-Discovery Workbook, $18.95
When Perfect Isn't Good Enough: Strategies for Coping with Perfectionism, $13.95
Earning Your Own Respect: A Handbook of Personal Responsibility, $12.95
High on Stress: A Woman's Guide to Optimizing the Stress in Her Life, $13.95
Infidelity: A Survival Guide, $13.95
Stop Walking on Eggshells, $14.95
Consumer's Guide to Psychiatric Drugs, $16.95
The Fibromyalgia Advocate: Getting the Support You Need to Cope with Fibromyalgia and Myofascial Pain, $18.95
Healing Fear: New Approaches to Overcoming Anxiety, $16.95
Working Anger: Preventing and Resolving Conflict on the Job, $12.95
Sex Smart: How Your Childhood Shaped Your Sexual Life and What to Do About It, $14.95
You Can Free Yourself From Alcohol & Drugs, $13.95
Amongst Ourselves: A Self-Help Guide to Living with Dissociative Identity Disorder, $14.95
Healthy Living with Diabetes, $13.95
Dr. Carl Robinson's Basic Baby Care, $10.95
Better Boundries: Owning and Treasuring Your Life, $13.95
Goodbye Good Girl, $12.95
Fibromyalgia & Chronic Myofascial Pain Syndrome, $19.95
The Depression Workbook: Living With Depression and Manic Depression, $17.95
Self-Esteem, Second Edition, $13.95
Angry All the Time: An Emergency Guide to Anger Control, $12.95
When Anger Hurts, $13.95

Call **toll free, 1-800-748-6273,** or log on to our online bookstore at **www.newharbinger.com** to order. Have your Visa or Mastercard number ready. Or send a check for the titles you want to New Harbinger Publications, Inc., 5674 Shattuck Ave., Oakland, CA 94609. Include $3.80 for the first book and 75¢ for each additional book, to cover shipping and handling. (California residents please include appropriate sales tax.) Allow two to five weeks for delivery.

Prices subject to change without notice.